Thine Is The Kingdom

A Biblical Perspective on the
Nature of Government and Politics Today

Paul Marshall

WILLIAM B. EERDMANS PUBLISHING COMPANY

Library of Congress Cataloging-in-Publication Data

Marshall, Paul.
Thine is the kingdom.

1. Christianity and politics.   2. Church and social
problems.   3. Politics in the Bible.   I. Title.
BR115.P7M3382   1986   261.7   85-27448

ISBN 0-8028-0174-9

Preface

Several years ago Philip Giddings complained that much Christian comment about politics was 'either pious generalities with which it would be difficult for anyone to disagree, or over-specific prescriptions which owe more to the author's political ideology than his Christian faith.' I think that this criticism was accurate and that it still is. Giddings suggested that one of the major things needed to correct this dismal situation was a 'framework' which would be 'sufficiently Christian to distinguish it from what is said by the political parties and media commentators, and also specific enough to be relevant to our immediate problems.'[1] I think that this need is still paramount and that Giddings' suggested 'framework' is vitally important.

Even though many evangelicals, especially younger ones, have now broken away from their long attachment to conservatism, they appear to have replaced their conservative views only with the common opinions of socialism. In this process there is often little evidence of seriously grappling with Scriptural teaching about political life. We are offered only generalizations about the unity and brotherhood of humankind, about the priority of concern for the poor and about the limits of private property. All these are certainly Scriptural, but they are hardly enough on which to build a political framework.

On the conservative side we are offered prescriptions based on the importance of individual freedom and responsibility and on the limits of government. These too are, I believe, Scriptural ideas, but they are scarcely enough to give political direction. Nor is it any real solution to be 'moderate' with respect to all the Scriptural demands and end up equating a Christian political framework with the Liberals or the Social Democrats. As any cursory reading of the Prophets or of the life of Jesus will show, 'moderation' (as distinct from humility) is not a very Christian virtue.

In this situation we need a framework for guiding Christian political action. This book is written as a beginning step in discovering and describing such a framework. No doubt this work too suffers from both 'pious generalities' and 'ideological prescriptions'. But I hope that it will help to move us in the right direction.

I have written primarily for an evangelical audience. While I hope that Christians (and non-Christians) other than evangelicals may benefit from it, the fact that I have assumed, rather than tried to prove, many of the assumptions of evangelicalism may mean that the book will mean less to others.

If we are to progress in our Christian political thinking and action we must be able to criticise each other's work and to move beyond it. Such criticism can be helped along if we know where each is coming from and, hence, the biases and blind spots we are likely to have. Consequently I think I ought to say something about my own background. I have been formed by mainstream evangelicalism, including Billy Graham, InterVarsity and the charismatic movement, and shaped by political work in Canada on such matters as native peoples, energy policy, social policy and human rights. This latter included work with and for evangelical groups, mainline churches, 'secular' political parties and lobbying organizations. Nevertheless, the major influence on my thinking has been the tradition of Christian politics developed over the last century in Dutch Calvinist circles, especially that associated with the names of Abraham Kuyper and Herman Dooyeweerd. I do not think that what is said in this book depends for its validity on such Calvinism, Dutch or otherwise, but the reader has a right to know something of what lies behind its writing.

Contents

Acknowledgements

I would like to thank my colleagues at and the supporters of the
Institute for Christian Studies for their encouragement and for
providing such a critical and exciting environment in which to
work. The staff and supporters of Citizens for Public Justice have
given both an example of Christian politics at work and also the
hope that Christian principles can work out into concrete and
healing policies. The Coalition for Christian Outreach, of Pitts-
burgh, allowed me to work out some of these ideas in a course
for their staff. Dorothe Rogers, Kathy Vanderkloet, Don
Knudsen and Jim Prall saw the manuscript through its typing
phases despite impossible author's deadlines. My thanks to Jim
Budd, Al Wolters, Bernard Zylstra, Gerald Vandezande and John
Peck for reading through and commenting on the manuscript. Of
course, none of these are responsible for any errors or other
absurdities in what follows. My wife Diane advised and encour-
aged me throughout, but she still doesn't like chapter 6.

1: Introduction

THE NATURE OF POLITICS

There are now very many and very good evangelical discussions of 'social action', 'social concern', 'caring for our neighbour', 'simple lifestyle', 'stewardship', and 'alternative community'. All of these matters are vitally important. All of them have particular implications for politics. No integrally Christian politics would be possible without them. But none of these matters is *per se* politics or political. When we talk about politics we are, if the dictionary and the history of the word are any guides, talking about things relevant to the actions of *governments*. We are talking about what governments do and what we do in relation to them.

Occasionally the term 'political' is used to refer to all 'power relations'. We hear of 'church politics', 'sexual politics', 'the politics of the family' and so forth. Occasionally we hear that everything is 'political', which might be true in a trivial way, but which is not very enlightening since it means just about the same as saying that nothing is political. If playing tiddlywinks and invading countries are both 'political', then the word can't mean very much that is important. We might as well say that everything is 'educational' or everything is 'sexual', which would be equally true and equally useless.

The reason why so many things are referred to as 'political' in this way is because they involve *power relations*. It is certainly true that politics involves power. But so do most other things in the creation. Sermons are, or should be, powerful, so should prayer, so should machines, arguments and books. But, as is clear from these examples, there is nothing specifically political about power. Politics involves a particular type of power, but that itself does not tell us what politics is.

There is one other meaning of 'politics' which is common. This is the idea of politics as double dealing, as bias, as lying, or at least shading, the truth (especially to help a political party). We speak of people 'playing politics', meaning that, rather than dealing openly and honestly with the matter at hand, they try to get some partisan advantage out of it. In this sense, a 'political' speech is one designed to make opponents look foolish. This is the understanding of politics beautifully portrayed in Ambrose Bierce's *The Devil's Dictionary*: 'POLITICS, n. A strife of interests masquerading as a contest of principles. The conduct of public affairs for private advantage'.[1]

I would be the last to deny that 'politics' in this sense makes up a vast amount of what modern governments and parties do. The Bible itself portrays these types of affairs with a clarity and a realism that would put Machiavelli to shame. As Samuel warned Israel:

> 'These will be the ways of the king who will reign over you. . . . He will take your daughters to be perfumers and cooks and bakers. He will take the best of your fields and vineyards and olive orchards and give them to his servants. He will take the tenth of your grain and of your vineyards and give it to his officers and to his servants. . . . And in that day you will cry out because of your king . . .' (1 Sam. 8:11–18).

But while politics is rife with sin such sin does not tell us what politics is, for government officials are also ministers of God (Romans 13:4). The tremendous power of politics to corrupt is simply a reflection of its tremendous power. This tendency to corruption should certainly cause us to be sceptical about all political claims, but it should not cause us to define politics by its corruption.

While, obviously, I can't force definitions on people, the present clear meaning of politics is to do with governments and states, what they are, what they do and what they should be doing. While matters such as simple lifestyle or directly helping our neighbours are vitally important, they are not what we will be discussing, except insofar as they affect the acts of governments and our acts towards governments. Christian books about politics, in this sense, are still comparatively rare.

Because we are concerned with politics it is not enough to suggest what may be good, or praiseworthy, or moral in people's conduct, unless we speak of the specific kind of goodness, the specific task, relevant to governments. Conversely we cannot assume that something evil, such as failing to love the Lord your God with all your heart, mind, soul and strength, is itself always a matter for government action or legal prohibition. We are concerned not with all types of good and evil but with those relevant to politics. We have to know, in a biblical way, something about what the *state* is supposed to do; what the *nature* and the *limits* of *political authority* and power are; what the *purpose* of *rulers*, 'God's servants', is; what the *function of law* is. We need not just a Christian understanding of life, nor just an understanding for Christian social action. We need a biblically inspired understanding of *politics*.

THE NEED FOR UNDERSTANDING

In the chapters that follow I focus on *understanding* politics rather than on concrete political action. This stress is quite deliberate. Certainly it is true that political events are urgent, even deadly. We are engaged in an arms race that threatens us all and consumes hundreds of billions of pounds. Around the world the sale and use of instruments of torture and death increases yearly. There is a proliferation of secular cults and ideologies which undermine any vision of truth capable of sustaining a healthy society. An increasing number of the world's poor starve to death daily and hourly.

I might also mention that most of my own work in the last several years has been practical in nature. It has been concentrated on current injustices and government policies to do with energy, poverty, and native peoples. I am strongly aware of the need for action. Hence I am not suggesting that Christian politics should be a kind of theological debating society. We have no need for scholastic quibbling whose end result is to avoid getting our hands dirty.

Nevertheless it is vital that we learn to *think* as we act. We cannot urge people to get 'involved' in politics unless we know the nature and purpose of that involvement. Otherwise we will end up reinforcing the injustices that presently exist because we will fall once again into existing patterns. If we consider some recent attempts at 'Christian politics' this should come home to us with a vengeance. In the 1980 Presidential election the United States had three candidates who each claimed to be born again and who each claimed that their policies were a reflection of their Christian commitment. Yet they each professed to disagree strongly with each other and to oppose one another's policies.

In the U.K. there isn't the same tendency among Christians to trumpet their own policies as *the* Christian way, but there still are trends similar to those in the U.S. Mrs. Thatcher maintains that she is upholding the traditional Christian morality of individual responsibility. Meanwhile a large segment of the Labour Party holds that the tenets of socialism – equality and brotherhood – are simply the political expression of Christianity. Among evangelicals there are divergent directions such as those illustrated by the Shaftesbury Project or the Festival of Light. There is a widespread tendency to take one aspect of Christian teaching, such as forgiveness of enemies, or human equality, or personal morality, or individual initiative, out of its context of redemption in Jesus Christ and, on the basis of that one aspect, to try to create a Christian political position. The result is that we end up with 'Christian' versions of almost every political ideology under the sun.

Clearly all of these 'Christian' positions are not true. Equally clearly, some 'Christian' politics undermines others. In such a situation we cannot get involved in politics as if kind hearts and good intentions are all we need. The road to hell, including political hells, is paved with good intentions. We cannot act in a healing way politically unless we have Christian principles. We can only learn such principles if we earnestly, critically, continually, systematically and prayerfully reflect on the biblical foundations of our politics. Anything less than this is not worthy of the need of our neighbours. R. H. Tawney, a Christian, active socialist and economic historian, expressed this well:

> Men may genuinely sympathize with the demand for a radical change. They may be conscious of social evils and sincerely anxious to remove them. They may set up a new department and appoint new officials, and invent a new name to express their resolution to effect something more drastic than reform, and less disturbing than revolution. But unless they take the pains, not only to act, but reflect, they end up by effecting nothing. For they deliver themselves bound to those who think they are practical, because they take their philosophy so much for granted as to be unconscious of its implications. As soon as they try to act, that philosophy re-asserts itself, and serves as an overriding force which presses their actions more deeply into the old channels.[2]

Similarly, as John Maynard Keynes pointed out, 'Practical men, who believe themselves to be quite exempt from any intellectual influences, are usually the slaves of some defunct economist.'[3] If you doubt this then read the headlines in your morning newspaper. There you will find recounted the acts committed by supposed practical men and women who are slaves of a defunct economist. That the defunct economist who lay behind most of this is the same John Maynard Keynes only reinforces the point.

Let me stress the same theme more broadly by quoting, if not the most influential, then certainly one of the most brilliant and perceptive of twentieth century Marxists, the Hungarian György Lukacs. He observed, accurately, that 'Lacking a theory, Marxists are condemned to trail along after daily events'.[4]

Lukacs' observations about Marxists can be applied equally well, better in fact, to Christians. If we are going to take the political problems of the world seriously, if we really intend to work against pain and suffering, then we have to know what we are doing. Running off half-cocked to denounce all manner of unrighteousness and to suggest all manner of 'solutions' is not going to help anybody.

In our work we must discover the resources of the whole body of Christ. Evangelicals have taken pains to point out great examples, such as Lord Shaftesbury or William Wilberforce, of evangelical political involvement in the past. But, despite such examples, it is clear that the political understanding and record of evangelicalism has been severely deficient. We still have much to learn. In doing such learning we cannot focus on only evangelical history or on only activities within the English speaking world.

Most of the deeper political thinking in the West, for the last one and a half millennia, has been by Christians seeking to be faithful in their politics. Origen and Augustine, Thomas Aquinas and John of Salisbury, John Calvin, Martin Luther and Menno Simons, Francisco Suarez, Richard Hooker, and John Locke – all of them sought, in their way, for a Christian approach to politics. There are many more recent examples: the French Thomist, Jacques Maritain, the Christian Democratic Parties of Latin America and of Europe (now the largest grouping in the European Parliament), Reinhold Niebuhr, the early Labour party in Britain, Abraham Kuyper and his followers in the Netherlands, Dietrich Bonhoeffer, the Social Credit or CCF in Canada, Solzhenitsyn. Or, considering the fact that now something like sixty percent of the world's Christians live in the third world, attempts by Christians in Zambia or Tanzania, or the developments of Liberation Theology and its western offshoots. Faced with such a breadth and such a history, we need more than Bible studies or urgings to Christian 'involvement'.

There are problems, often grave ones, with many of the people and movements I have just listed. But we are fools if we believe that we can act strategically in politics without an awareness of what others have thought, and said, and done. Being in the European Economic Community, we must start learning from the Christian Democratic parties in Europe, especially the major Calvinist-influenced one in the Netherlands. Many of these parties

have degenerated into pragmatism but, often, their Christian
political awareness is far more developed than anything in the
U.K. In the light of the Scriptures we must sift and learn from
their work. To quote Marx: 'Ignorance never helped anybody' –
not even Christians.

AVOIDING MORALISM

The fact that we are focussing on politics should keep us from
'moralism'. If all that is meant by 'morality' is that politics always
and inevitably involves choices about good and evil, justice and
injustice, then I have no quarrel with moralism, for no political
action is a purely 'technical' or 'expert' matter. But in politics we
must be concerned with more than morality in general. We must
talk about a particular type of morality – that of governments and
states. It is not enough to know that some things, such as wife
battering or pornography, are bad, we have to know whether they
are properly matters for government action and we have to
grapple with the judicial minefields of family legislation and
censorship.

Nor can we even speak in an abstract way of what would be
'moral' for governments to do, such as banning trade with South
Africa or with the Soviet Union. Each of these actions has
particular consequences, many of them unintended, and many of
them bad. These consequences will vary depending on how the
policy is carried out. Each policy will have effects on other policies
both in the U.K. and in other countries. We have to know if we
can accept these consequences. If we take *politics* in God's world
seriously then it is with *these* types of questions that we must
grapple. Morality must become *concrete political morality*.

Similarly we must not think that something has to be immoral
in the first place for governments to do something about it. Some
actions, such as driving through a red light, are quite alright if
there isn't a law against them. Laws can be regulations of things
which are not wrong in themselves but whose regulation would
achieve a good public purpose. Once the law is passed, that action
takes on a whole new context and *then* becomes a matter of
political morality.

Above all we should not treat all questions of politics as if they
were ultimately rooted in the *personal* morality of those involved.
Certainly there is wickedness in politics and we must say so. But,
though we may seek to be directed by the word of God, we can
have no *presumption* that our opponents are more wicked than
us, nor that bad politics necessarily boils down to deficiency of
character.

Moralism in this last sense is widespread, even amongst those who claim to be purely pragmatic politicians. Despite the efforts of Mrs. Thatcher, who has contributed more than her fair share to this disease, such moralism still seems to be a major preoccupation of the political left. It is often implied, for example, that one of the major reasons for our horrendous unemployment is that Mrs. Thatcher, Sir Geoffrey Howe or Nigel Lawson are inherently less compassionate and concerned for the poor than are Roy Hattersley, Tony Benn or Neil Kinnock.

I have no idea whether these accusations are true or not. Quite frankly, I don't much care one way or the other, for the basic point is that these are not, *per se*, political issues. The political issue is whether the policies of the Tories, or Labour, or the Alliance, can be carried out and, if so, are they genuinely going to help the unemployed or not. Mrs. Thatcher's argument is that unless the British economy is streamlined and revitalised, which is a painful process, then the number and lot of the unemployed will be far worse in the future. It is this argument that must be tackled. The essential point is that it is the *policies* and *programmes*, not the personal characteristics of their promoters, that must be addressed and criticised. If the policies do in fact pass muster then we should support them. There is little political point, though there are other points, in calling Mrs. Thatcher (or David Owen or David Steel or Neil Kinnock) to repentance unless that repentance involved a turning to a Christian understanding of politics and economics. And that, in turn, requires that we have some understanding of what Christian politics and economics look like. 'Concern for the unemployed', even, or especially, in the hearts and minds of Christians, will just be political demoguery unless it is harnessed to a genuine and integrally Christian understanding of the way the economies of countries function.

Similarly, though we should certainly do so, it is not enough to criticise greed, militarism, racism, pollution, or whatever, as if these were just evils, even structured evils, perpetrated by vile and wicked people. We must be concerned with the actual systems, structures, policies and ideologies which enshrine and continue such evils. We need to know about the structure and dynamics of capitalism, about the military in terms of geopolitics, about the innate tendencies of powerful state bureaucracies, about the arms industry's place in the economy, about the psychological and sociological factors of racism. We need to deal with them in terms which are politically relevant. This is part, at least, of what the Apostle Paul means when he says:

For we wrestle not against flesh and blood, but against principalities and powers, against the rulers of this present darkness, against the spiritual host of wickedness in heavenly places (Eph. 6:17).

Because we must address political rather than personal matters, we cannot assume that we can deal with political problems merely by encouraging large numbers of compassionate evangelical Christians to go into politics. The effect of such people would depend, in large part, on what their political principles are. Many of the inhabitants of Northern Ireland, the southern United States and the Republic of South Africa do *not* rejoice in the fact that they are blessed, or cursed, with the proximity of large numbers of very upright, very pious, theologically conservative politicians. Many of their problems stem from such people.

It is not enough to urge good things or have good intentions. We need coherent commitments and policies that deal with our concrete situations. One of the facts of modern politics is that our opponents are often no more sinful than we are. We must not pretend otherwise.

OUTLINE OF BOOK

In chapter 2 I try to describe what Christian action in God's world is. My purpose is to show that the task given to humankind by God at the creation has not ended due to sin but rather is continued in a renewed way through redemption in Jesus Christ. The fall has sorely corrupted the world, but it has not caused the world to pass away from God's law and preserving order. Through Jesus Christ not only people, not only souls, but all of the creation can be and will be reconciled to God and, hence, with itself. Unless we understand the overall scope of our Christian task, then our politics will become only a sideline to evangelism or else an impossible quest for a utopia. To understand our task we must begin where the Bible does, with God's creation of and ordering of the world in which we live. We must also end where the Bible does, with the vision of the kings of the earth bringing their glory into the New Jerusalem. In between we live in the struggle between good and evil throughout the whole creation. We live with the reality of sin but we seek and expect the righteousness and justice of God.

In Chapter 3 I outline the development in the Bible of the political order as the authority which God has set up to establish just relations between persons and groups. We will consider the purpose for which government has been made and the meaning of justice, which it is to uphold. Government is only one of the authorities on the earth and, because it always stands alongside other authorities that God has ordained, it can never try to become a law unto itself or require absolute obedience. Government is, in fact, a task given to all humankind, for we are all responsible for establishing just relations between us.

In Chapter 4 I suggest how we can move from what the Bible says in order to arrive at guidelines for Christian political action in the modern age. We will consider how we can judge unions, corporations, parliaments, or elections even though they are not things with which the Bible deals. I also emphasize that Christian action is free action, it always requires real responsibility in the ongoing development of new Christian approaches. This responsibility also means that we can have no 'magic' solutions to world problems. We look at *political analysis* – how we can understand the forces at play in the world, at *idolatry* as one key to understanding what happens in politics, at the place of *law* in politics, and at how governments should approach questions of *morality*.

Chapters 5 and 6 examine two current political questions in the light of the guidelines developed in chapter 4. The two examples are economics and the welfare state (chapter 5) and international relations and the nuclear arms race (chapter 6). I consider only *two* issues because, if we are to understand any current political issue in anything more than a shallow and trivial way, then we need to know something of its history and dynamics, and also the complexities of proposed solutions. Even so, these two chapters are still quite superficial. The reasons I have taken *these two* issues are that they are urgent ones, they are ones which are currently at the top of the political agenda, they are ones rooted in many of the non-Christian dynamics of our age, and they deal with many technical matters, thus showing that Christian politics must be and can be more than just a focus on 'moral' questions. Understanding the welfare state and nuclear arms requires more background and biblical materials than have been outlined so far and so in chapter 5 I introduce biblical teaching on the nature of economics and on the place of the poor, while in chapter 6 I introduce material on war.

In chapter 7 I close with some guidelines for the *manner* of Christian political action: that it is a communal, not an individual task; that it is not particularly a task for the institutional church but rather one for the laity, the body of Christ in the world; and that it is oriented not toward achieving goals but to *following a path* in humility and obedience. Finally I try to set our political task in the context of eschatology, the pattern of the end times, pointing out both the fear and the hope that the final coming of the Kingdom of God should instil within us.

2: Christian Action in God's World

CREATION

The Cultural Mandate

In Genesis 1:28 God says to the first man and woman: 'Be fruitful and multiply, and fill the earth, and subdue it'. This often is referred to as 'the cultural mandate' – God's instruction to humankind to develop culture and science and society upon the earth. This mandate receives relatively little attention in Christian circles. Occasionally its significance is denied because it took place before the fall had radically altered the human situation, and so it is thought to be of little significance to us now. More often it is affirmed as something that God still requires of us, but then it recedes into insignificance in relation to the 'gospel mandate' as expressed by, for example, Matthew: 'Go therefore and make disciples of all nations, baptizing them in the name of the Father and of the Son and of the Holy Spirit, teaching them to observe all that I have commanded you . . .' (28:19–20). Compared to this command the cultural mandate is often treated as an aside which might be true but which is not central. It is treated as almost optional.

But the cultural mandate and the gospel mandate are not meant to substitute for each other: we do not have to choose between one and the other. Nor should we even say (as do so many Christians who wrestle with the problem of 'evangelism and social action') that these mandates should be *added* to one another. Rather, we must see these two mandates as essentially two aspects of the same thing – that we are servants and followers of God through Jesus Christ in whatever we think or feel or do in any and every area of God's creation. This becomes clear when we see the full significance of the cultural mandate, and this significance can be seen if we look at that mandate in its full context.[1]

This command of God to the first man and woman, and through them to all of us, comes as the culmination of the story of God's creation of the earth. The story of the creation (Gen. 1:1–2:3) forms a clearly marked off literary whole which is plainly meant to be understood as a unit. It opens with the declaration that God created both the heavens and the earth. The focus then shifts to the earth. We are told how, through eight creative words, God produces the present, varied structure of the world out of that which was at first 'without form and void'. On the first day darkness is separated from light, night from day. On the second day the waters above and below are separated. On the third day the lower waters are divided into dry land and sea, and then the land is filled with vegetation. On the fourth day God makes the lights appear in the heaven, the sun, the moon and the stars. On the fifth day God fills the air and sea with birds and fishes.

This description of God's acts on the first five days is not haphazard, as if God has worked at whim. The story shows a definite progression as God works and shapes, gradually building the earth which was planned from the beginning. God's acts on the sixth day are not just the last acts on the list before the seventh day of rest: rather, they are the *culmination* of God's purpose, the *climax* of what God is doing. The sixth day is the day that tells us the point of the whole exercise. On this day God creates the animals and then man and woman. Having made them, God says to them, as the last act in the drama of creation, that they must 'be fruitful' and tells them that they 'have dominion over the fish of the sea and over the birds of the air and over every living thing that moves upon the earth'. The cultural mandate is presented as the climax of the story of creation itself. The mandate shows God's purpose. After the man and woman are given their task, after they have been told what they were made for, then the work of creation has been completed. God now pronounces it good and takes a rest.

Not only the timing but also the *way* that God creates the man and the woman is significant. In all the other acts of creation God says, 'let there be . . . and it was so'. But on the sixth day we are told, for the first time, of God *planning* the creation of humankind (v. 26), and *then* carrying out the plan (v. 28). We are also told what God's plan is. The plan is to make humankind 'to be our image and to have dominion'. Thus 'having dominion' is itself part of God's creative act; it is built into the very way that God makes the world. The 'cultural mandate' is part of God's plan of world creation. Human moulding of the earth is the continuation of God's creative acts.

The cultural mandate also shows something of what it means

that we are made 'in the image' of God. To be in the image of
God is to be like God in some way. There are several expressions
of this image – the New Testament mentions righteousness,
holiness, and knowledge. In Genesis the image seems specifically
to refer to lordship, to having dominion over the creation. Genesis
1:26 reads, 'Let us make humankind in our own image, after our
likeness; and let them have dominion . . .'. It is better translated,
'Let us make humankind in our image . . . *in order that* they
might have dominion'. This is the same theme as found in the
Psalms: 'Thou hast given him dominion over the works of Thy
hands, Thou hast put all things under his feet' (Ps. 8:5–6). One
way of being like God is to have dominion over the earth, to be
stewards of the creation, to be fruitful. When we fulfil God's
purpose in making the world and in making us, then we are
manifesting the image of God.

In summary, the immediate context of the cultural mandate is
its position as the climax and focus of God's creative work. The
works of the previous days, the command to multiply and have
dominion, the creation of humankind as God's image, God's
ceasing and resting after the giving of the mandate – everything
highlights the importance of the command that God has given us.
The beginning of the Bible, God's written revelation to us, is
focussed in telling us who we are and why God has made us. We
are those who are called to image God by our activities in shaping
and forming the materials of God's creation.

The Development of Human Culture

The cultural mandate is further illuminated by what follows in
Genesis and the mandate in turn provides the context and the
prologue for what follows. The first chapter of Genesis is like a
stage setting. In the first five days the lights, the scenery and the
props are put into place. On the sixth day the actors, the hero
and the heroine, are introduced and the theme of the script is
announced. The context for the drama has now been given, and
the drama itself can begin. The drama which follows is all the
actions of humankind, God's stewards, on the earth, God's
creation. The drama is human history itself.

The pattern of the drama is shown by the structure of the book
of Genesis. Genesis divides itself into eleven sections. The first
section is the prologue which we have just described. Each of the
other sections is distinguished and introduced by the words: 'these
are the generations of . . .'. Gen. 2:4 says 'These are the generations of the heavens and the earth once they had been created'.
Gen. 5:1 begins 'the book of the generations of Adam'. Gen.

6:9 announces 'These are the generations of Noah'. This pattern continues through 'the generations of' the sons of Noah (10:1), Shem (11:10), Terah (11:27), Ishmael (25:12), Isaac (25:19), Esau (36:1) and Jacob (37:2). This is how Genesis describes its own structure.

The accounts of the 'begettings', the 'generations', include genealogies, lists of actual generations of parents and children, but they also include far more than this. The account of generations includes the fall (3:6), casting out from Eden (3:23), murder (6:8), the beginning of cities (4:17), the development of herding and nomadic life (4:20), music (4:21), tools (4:22) and so forth.

The story of Genesis tells in summary form *all* that the children of Adam 'begot', all that they 'brought forth'. We are told of the birth of human culture, of technology, of agriculture, and we are told of the effects of human sin. These 'generations' are what we would call human history. The structure of Genesis is centred around an account of human beings as the *shapers of history*: it tells us what those who have been called to fill and subdue the earth actually have done in response to this command, whether sinfully, as with Cain, or obediently, as with Noah. After we have been told what human life in obedience to God, in the image of God, is all about, and after God has set the stage for human history, then Genesis shows what the actors do on that stage in response to the mandate.

Although because of sin human beings act in evil ways, yet even in that evil way they *still* respond to this mandate, they *still* tend animals, they build, they make music, they spread across the earth. Genesis recounts the life of humankind as they respond to the basic command that God has given them. As this history unfolds God continues to aid, to guide, to reward and to punish human actions. After Noah has landed the ark, he is henceforth allowed to eat the flesh of animals (9:3), a thing which was not allowed earlier (1:30). The story of the tower of Babel recounts the development of brickmaking and tar but, because the tower was an effort to *avoid* the cultural mandate of being 'scattered abroad upon the face of the whole earth' then God subsequently scatters the builders abroad (11:1–8).

This structure of Genesis as a pattern of generations also shows why the account of Adam and Eve given in 2:4 onwards should not be treated as a second account of creation, as some scholars do. This section is called the generations of the heavens and earth. It is the unfolding of what has gone before. It begins the history after the stage has been set. It shows what Adam and Eve do in response to what God has said to them. Certainly there is an overlap with what is described in Genesis 1, but the same events are now related with a new focus, that of showing the actual outworking of the cultural mandate. Genesis 2 picks up the details in order to show what Adam and Eve 'brought forth'.

The Cultural Mandate Throughout the Bible

There is one other context in which the 'cultural mandate' should be understood, that of the Bible as a whole. We know that the Word of God tells us more and more as it develops. The New Testament reveals more than the Old, and Jesus is the revelation of more than has been told before. In this sense the Bible progresses, it moves onward, in its revelation. But this progress never rejects what has gone before. The Bible adds, deepens, refines and clarifies, but it does not turn aside. The 'cultural mandate' is not something rejected as the biblical story of redemption unfolds. Rather, the mandate is fleshed out and placed in the context of the whole life of humankind through the fall and through redemption in Jesus Christ. Right through the Scriptures God keeps calling people back to their task.

When God gives a law to the people of Israel, its precepts are not devoted exclusively to so-called 'spiritual' concerns. The law is designed to cover all of the dimensions of Israel's relations with God, with one another and with the earth. Detailed instructions are given for their politics and economics, matters to which we shall return in chapter 3. Rules and guides are laid down for marriage and family life. There are also laws to govern what sorts of food they should eat (Lev. 11), how to build safe houses (Deut. 22:8), how to care for the land (Lev. 25:1–7), how to treat animals (Deut. 22:6), how to maintain health (Lev. 12–15), even how to be hygienic when using the bathroom (Deut. 23:12–13). In the construction of the tabernacle we read '. . . the Lord has called Bezalel . . . and he has filled him with the Spirit of God, with ability, with intelligence, with all knowledge and with all craftsmanship, to devise artistic designs, to work in gold and silver and bronze, in cutting stones for setting, and in carving wood, for work in every skilled craft . . . He has filled [him] with ability . . .' (Ex. 35:30–35).

Nor is this merely an Old Testament theme which is replaced in the New Testament. It is simply not true that the Old Testament deals with what is external whereas the New Testament deals with what is internal. It is not true that the Old Testament focusses on works whereas the New focusses on faith. Redemption in both Testaments is always rooted in the grace of God, never in human works. Equally true is the fact that obedience to God, as service, as loving response and as thanks, is always manifested in every area and type of activity in the creation. This is shown in, for example, the Apostle Paul's comments about work.

Paul criticised idleness and exhorted Christians to work (cf. 2 Thess. 3:6). He made no distinctions between physical and spiritual work, in fact he used the same terms to refer both to the manual labour by which he earned a living and also to his apostolic service (1 Cor. 4:12; 15:10; 16:16; Eph. 4:28; Romans 10:12; Gal. 4:11; Phil. 2:16; Col. 1:29; 1 Thess. 5:12). Often it is quite difficult to know to which he was referring, or whether he himself was making such a distinction. For Paul, all the different types of work originated in faith and were service to God. When he outlines the service of the 'new nature . . . created after the likeness of God', he urges 'doing honest work with his hands'. Clearly the new nature in Christ is not some disembodied creature. The new person, restored in Christ, is to work in God's world, to supply the needs of others, to shape the development of human life (Eph. 4:17–32, esp. v. 28; 2 Cor. 11:9; 12:13; 1 Thess. 4:9–12; 2 Thess. 3:8; Acts 20:35). As in Genesis, the image, the likeness of God, is related also to human activity in the creation.

What Paul writes about work is in radical contrast to the attitudes of the surrounding world.[2] In Greek culture, the manual worker was despised as one bound by necessity, he was considered a part-slave. In such culture the only life deemed worth living was a life freed from necessary work in order to pursue recreation, politics, philosophy or religion. But Paul did not regard religion as a 'spiritual' activity separate from work. He regarded all aspects of life as equally religious when done in service to God. He called Christians to manifest the image of God through their day to day work.

The rediscovery of this view of work was one of the major accomplishments of the Reformation. In contrast to medieval Catholicism, which had elevated the contemplative life above all others, the Reformers emphasised that the priesthood of all believers meant that all of human service was equally service to God. Luther wrote:

> If you are a manual labourer, you find that the Bible has been put into your workshop, into your hand, into your heart. It teaches and preaches how you should treat your neighbour . . . just look at your tools . . . at your needle and thimble, your beer barrel, your goods, your scales or yardstick or measure . . . and you will read this statement inscribed in them. Everywhere you look, it stares at you. . . . You have as many preachers as you have transactions, goods, tools and other equipment in your house and home.[3]

ƐſƐᲣᎤ

One of the articles of heresy for which William Tyndale, the father
of the English Bible, was convicted was that he had said: 'There
is no work better than another to please God: to pour water, to
wash dishes, to be a souter (cobbler) or an apostle, all is one; to
wash dishes and to preach is all one, as touching the deed, to
please God'.[4]

The story of creation and the giving of the cultural mandate is
not some obscure part of Scripture given merely for the sake of
historical interest. Nor does it refer only to what God wanted of
people in some bygone age. Nor is it something apart from Christian faith. It shows that humankind is not a set of apprentice
angels who are only suited to existence on another spiritual plane
(see also Heb. 2:5–9). We are the ones whom God has made for
the earth and charged with the task of shepherding the world, of
serving God in our day to day tasks, of loving God and one
another in whatever we do.

THE FALL

When we describe the God-given purpose of human beings in
terms of the 'cultural mandate', we, of course, are passing over
many things. The most obvious thing we have neglected to
mention so far is the fact of the fall and of sin. Immediately after
the drama of human history begins, as the first of the 'generations',
that of 'the heavens and the earth', unfolds, the man and the
woman corrupt the whole enterprise by falling out of relationship
with God. After the fall the unfolding of the generations is always
marked by evil, by corruption and by distortion.

When they eat of the fruit of the tree, the man and the woman
become separated from God (Gen. 3:8). This results in them
becoming separated from each other: Adam turns against Eve
and blames her for what happened (3:12). Because of his sin he
begins to dominate her (3:16). Even the earth then becomes
corrupt and turns against them: 'cursed is the ground because of
you; in toil you shall eat of it all the days of your lives; thorns
and thistles it shall bring forth to you . . .' (3:17–18). Even the
act of begetting the further generations becomes tainted: 'in pain
you shall bring forth children' (3:16). Paul describes this whole
process as 'death spread to all men' (Romans 5:12) and the 'reign
of death' (Romans 5:21) in which 'the creation was subjected to
futility' and 'bondage to decay' so that 'the whole creation has
been groaning in travail' (Romans 8:20–22).

This fast spreading circle of the effects of sin shows the vast
consequences of the scope of the dominion that humans have.
Precisely because we are the ones who are to steward the earth,

our sin has effects throughout the whole of the earth. *Every* relationship becomes corrupted. As humans are to fill the earth, then no part of the earth remains immune from the effects of our sin. We are separated from God, from one another, and from the world about us.

But despite these catastrophic effects, the fall did not end the cultural mandate. Eve still brings forth the generations, Adam still works the ground. In fact they cannot stop fulfilling this task, for that is how God has made them and us. Even though we are fallen, we do not cease to work, or play, or pray, or bring up children, or make political decisions. We *have* to do these things, this is how God has made us. This task is an aspect of our imaging God and we cannot even survive if we do not fulfil it.

The mandate given to Adam and Eve, and through them to us, has not ended. But we have failed to follow it in loving and obedient ways. We carry out the same tasks, but we perform those tasks in evil and corrupt ways. We misuse God's gifts, we exploit the earth and one another for the sake of greed and pride. Because of sin the drama of filling the earth and shaping our human life together has become one filled with suffering and injustice. In fact, it often seems to be the case that those most inclined to sin have taken the lead in shaping the earth. It is Cain, the first murderer, who builds the first city and whose children begin work with tools and music. The first use of bricks and tar is to build a great tower at Babel 'to make a name for ourselves' and defy the Lord (Gen. 11:4). Israel's first call for a king comes from their desire to imitate their warlike neighbours (1 Sam. 3:4–22).

Despite this evil misuse of God's good gifts, the mandate continues. God continues in mercy to provide for humankind and to direct them in the right way to fulfil their responsibility. Immediately after the curse, perhaps in pity for their miserable leaves, 'God made for Adam and for his wife garments of skins, and clothed them' (Gen. 3:21). God gives aid to Eve to bring forth children (4:1), and provides another child to replace the one she had lost (4:25). God hears the cry of Abel's blood (4:10), and even preserves Abel's murderer, Cain (4:15). Noah, who found favour with the Lord, is announced with the words, 'Out of the ground which the Lord has cursed this one shall bring us relief from our work and from the toil of our hands' (5:29). With Noah God mitigates the effects of the toil which come with sin.

The story of Noah tells how God determined to do something about the way in which people were corrupting the earth and perverting their task: 'God saw the earth, and behold, it was corrupt; for all flesh had corrupted their way upon the earth'

(6:12). God decides to end the violence and to save a remnant who can carry out their task properly. When Noah and his family and the animals are saved, God speaks to them before they disperse over the earth. What God says here is a reiteration of the mandate given at the dawn of creation. Even after the fall the saved remnant are told to 'be fruitful and multiply, bring forth abundantly on the earth and multiply in it' (9:7). To make this task easier God now allows Noah's children to eat meat (9:3), whereas before humankind had been restricted to eating plant life (1:29, 30). This is one way in which the promised 'relief from the toil of our hands' was brought about.

Whereas the story of the generations of Adam shows the spreading effect of sin, the story of the generations of Noah shows that even after the fall God still has the same purpose in mind for the stewards of the earth. Humankind is given new help and a fresh start and is set about its life task once more. God establishes a covenant that never again shall the earth be destroyed by flood and points to the rainbow as the sign of the covenant. This covenant is made not only with Noah and his descendants but also 'with every living creature that is with you, the birds, the cattle, and every beast of the earth with you, as many as came out of the ark' (9:10). The rainbow is a sign between God 'and every living creature of all flesh' (9:12, 15, 16, 17). God cares for and keeps faith with all of the creation. God is committed to the preservation of the earth and to the ongoing process of human history.

With Noah the cycle of human culture begins once more and immediately we read that 'Noah was the first tiller of the soil' (9:20), and that from his children 'the whole earth was peopled' (9:19). From these children 'the coastland peoples spread' (10:5). From them came Nimrod 'the first on earth to be a mighty man. He was a mighty hunter before the Lord' (10:8, 9). The spread and the activity of the human population is traced and, for a while, it seems as though people are taking up their task in responsible and healing ways. People like Nimrod have learned how hunting is to be done properly and they do their task 'before the Lord'. But people go astray once again and pervert their energies into the construction of the tower of Babel so that the Lord intervenes and scatters them abroad.

The earliest chapters of Genesis reveal a pattern. God sets us in the world as bearers of the divine image with a task to do. We have fallen into sin, and perverted this task. But God, who is continually gracious and merciful, helps us and directs us back onto our path. Sin corrupts us but it does not change our calling. We are still those whom God calls to be the stewards of the earth. Our obedience to God is still manifested in our service in all dimensions of our earthly, human existence. Human history under God's hand still goes on.

REDEMPTION

The Promise to Abraham and Sarah

After the story of the tower of Babel, Genesis moves on rapidly and lists the succeeding generations without much comment until we come to the account of the generations of Terah (11:27). Terah lived in Ur of the Chaldees but later took his family to Haran. It is in Haran that God once again sets out to bring humankind back to the truth and to redirect their paths. God appears to one of Terah's children, the one we now call Abraham. 'The Lord said to Abram "Go from your country and your kindred and your father's house to the land that I will show you. And I will make of you a great nation, and I will bless you, and make your name great, so that you will be a blessing. I will bless those who bless you, and him who curses you I will curse; and in you all the families of the earth will be blessed" ' (12:1–3). Paul describes this promise as God saying to Abram 'that his descendants should inherit the world' (Romans 4:13).

After the fall of the first man and woman and the spread of sin throughout the earth, after the new beginning with Noah had degenerated to Babel, God calls out Abram and Sarah (17:16) and reveals to them a plan for the blessing of all the families of the world. God's plan of redemption is being revealed – through Abram and Sarah will come the One who will forgive human sins, set humankind at right with God, and lead all creatures into paths of peaceful, loving service. God intimates the coming of Jesus Christ, who will heal the effects of sin throughout the world. As Paul says:

> Therefore as sin came into the world through one man and death through sin, and so death spread to all men because all men sinned . . . much more have the grace of God and the free gift in the grace of that one man Jesus Christ abounded for many (Romans 5:12, 15).

All of Genesis to this point has been a narrowing of focus. From the drama of the heavens and earth we move closer in order to see the history of humankind. From the history of humankind we move closer to see the history of the children of Shem, the Semites. From the history of the Semites we move closer to see the history of Abraham and Sarah. Through the narrative of the effects of sin and the struggling attempts of humankind to fulfil the mandate that God has given them, the story has become concentrated on God's plan to undo the effects of sin, to redeem humankind and make it what it has been called to be.

With the introduction of the children of Abraham and Sarah, the Scriptures now focus on the drama of God's redemption. This is the story that fills the rest of the Bible. We follow the chosen nation, Israel, whom God will save, cherish, guide and instruct in the Law about the right way to live as children of God. From this nation, which God has chosen to be the bearer of good news to the world, will come the Messiah, the One who will bring God's love and forgiveness to all the peoples of the earth. The Bible is the story of how sin has been, is being, and will be overcome through Jesus Christ. It is the story of how humankind has and will be redeemed and restored to fellowship with God. The creatures whom God has made to love and have dominion of the earth will be brought back to that. This is what *redemption* means – to bring back, to buy back. The Bible is given to us to tell us this message.

Daniel and the Promise to the Nations

The history of Israel is the history of the people whom God has chosen and with whom God has covenanted (promised). God saves Israel from Egypt and teaches them how to live, how to divide up the land, how to make decisions about marriage, how to bring up children, how to handle and punish murder and theft. Gradually it becomes clear to Israel that God wants not just them but *all* nations to live in the manner that Israel is supposed to live. This becomes clear in the book of Daniel.

Daniel takes place when Israel has been defeated and its leaders have been taken in exile to Babylon. Daniel and his friends have been uprooted and transported to the centre of the world's greatest city and greatest empire. In terms of world politics Daniel came from a provincial backwater of a country. Israel was small, with hardly enough people to make it worth the time for a mighty empire to invade it. Israel's major claim for attention was that it stood across major routes connecting the centres of world civilisation. Except for a relatively small expansion under David and Solomon, Israel was a buffer state between the competing claims of Egypt, Assyria and Babylon. From out of this obscure place, remarkable only for the fact that its people were obsessed with the idea that their God was the God over all gods and that they were a chosen people, Daniel rises to be an adviser to the world's greatest empire. But Daniel wants to remain faithful to the Lord and he struggles to discover how God wants him to advise this empire. In the book of Daniel we see the redemptive purposes of God now being played out on a vaster stage – the relations between the nations of all the then known world.

Gradually Daniel realises that this whole world is in God's hands. After God speaks to him concerning Nebuchadnezzar's dream, Daniel exclaims 'He changes times and seasons; he removes kings and sets up kings . . .' (Dan. 2:20). Nebuchadnezzar himself says 'Truly, your God is God of gods and Lord of Kings . . .' (2:47). This theme is repeated throughout the book: 'His kingdom is an everlasting kingdom, and His dominion is from generation to generation' (4:3). At the end of his life, Nebuchadnezzar realises the same thing 'for his dominion is an everlasting dominion, and his kingdom endures from generation to generation . . .' (4:34). Daniel points out to King Belshazzar 'the Most High God gave Nebuchadnezzar your father kingship and greatness and glory and majesty . . . but when his heart was lifted up and his spirit was hardened so that he dealt proudly, he was deposed . . . until he knew that the Most High God rules over the kingdom of men . . . And you his son, Belshazzar . . . the God in whose hand is your breath, and whose are all your ways, you have not honoured' (5:18–23). Later even Darius the Great decreed, 'He is the living God, enduring for ever; his kingdom shall never be destroyed, and his dominion shall be to the end' (6:26).

This is the continual theme of Daniel – that God is the God not only of Israel, but of the whole earth. That God's dominion (also expressed, as we have seen, through the dominion of God's people) still goes on throughout history – from generation to generation. It does not stop after the generations listed in Genesis. God's dominion covers all kingdoms, all empires, indeed it covers the whole earth. Ultimately these kingdoms will pass into God's own kingdom of love and righteousness. As the people of Israel spill over onto the world stage, so it becomes clear that God is the God and the Redeemer of the world. What God plans to do he will do not only for Israel, but also for Babylon, for Rome, and for whatever follows. Daniel tells us that God's purposes in choosing Israel are ones that take in the whole world, that God's dominion continues and will not cease.

Paul's Letters

The Apostle Paul reiterates this theme in Romans. After showing the significance of Abraham (chapter 4), and after proclaiming that what one man, Adam, corrupted will be restored in one man, Jesus Christ, (chapter 5), Paul describes the effect of sin and the place of the law and of faith (chapters 6 & 7). Then in chapter 8 he announces that 'the law of the Spirit of life in Christ Jesus has set me free from the law of sin and death' (8:1), and he shows how the just requirements of the law might now be fulfilled (8:4). Because of this we are now children of God, who cry 'Abba! Father!', and are heirs of God (8:15–17). Not content to let the matter rest there, Paul rushes on to show the full significance of this restoration as children of God – that it is *a promise to the creation itself*. 'For the creation waits with eager longing for the revelation of the sons of God; for the creation was subject to futility, not of its own will but by the will of him who subjected it in hope; because the creation itself will be set free from its bondage to decay and obtain the glorious liberty of the children of God. We know that the whole creation has been groaning in travail together until now, and not only the creation, but we ourselves, who have the first fruits of the spirit, groan inwardly as we wait for adoption as sons, the redemption of our bodies' (8:19–23).

In this glorious climax announcing the liberty in the Spirit of the children of God, Paul says that this is not all – the creation itself suffers because of the effects of the sin of its stewards, the creation itself waits eagerly for freedom from oppression, the creation itself will be set free just as (and because) the children of God are set free. Paul exults that God's redemption is for the creation – everything that God has made. The restoration of humankind, those whom God has set over the earth to tend and fill it, ultimately means, through the renewing of their task, the restoration of the world itself. That is why 'nothing in all creation will be able to separate us from the love of God in Christ Jesus our Lord' (8:39).

Paul does not mean that each and every individual thing, or even each and every individual person, will be saved, for he directly goes on to talk about God's election, God's choice of some. His point is not that every *individual* thing will be saved but that all sorts of things will be saved. Just as sin has affected everything, so also redemption will affect everything. Redemption in Jesus Christ is not limited to any one area of the creation. Not only persons, but nations, kingdoms, the entire creation will be reconciled. God, through Jesus Christ, will make a new heaven and a new earth wherein righteousness dwells. God will make *all things new* (Rev. 21:5).

Paul sums all of this up by proclaiming: 'for from him and through him and to him are all things' (Romans 11:36), and he then tells the Church at Rome what this redemption means for how they must now live. He tells them to 'present their *bodies* as a *living* sacrifice' and that this *living* sacrificial life is itself 'spiritual worship' (12:1). He tells them to judge their abilities and gifts soberly (12:3) and that they have different gifts, so that each will do a different type of thing in the restoration of creation (12:6–8). He tells them that they are not just individuals but that they are 'individually members one of another'. The new people in Christ are members of a body fitted together, who have a communal task in the world (12:4–5). Paul goes on to give advice for those with different kinds of gifts – prophets, administrators, teachers, preachers, almsgivers, officials, doers of works of mercy (12:6, 7). He tells them how to do these tasks, hating evil, loving good, with zeal, patience, constancy in prayer, generosity, tears, rejoicing, harmony, humility, forgiveness, and peacefulness (12:9–20). They must not be conformed to the patterns of the age they live in but be transformed as the forerunners and first fruits of the new age (12:2).[5] The Christian task in the world is summed up in the words 'Do not be overcome with evil, but overcome evil with good' (12:21) – withstand and reverse the effects of sin, overcome evil so that love and righteousness and peace may prevail in the world.

Having given general instruction for God's new people in their service in God's world, Paul turns his attention to particular examples of service. He tells them what to do in relation to government (13:1–7), debts (13:8), the law (13:8–10), eating taboos (14:1–4), special days (14:5–9) and judgements (14:10–14). He points out that 'nothing is unclean in itself' (14:14), that is, that there is nothing in the creation which is, in and of itself, a forbidden thing for Christian use or a forbidden area for Christian service.

This theme is repeated in others of Paul's letters, most strongly in the letter to the Colossians. Paul, perhaps quoting an early Christian hymn, says of Christ, that:

He is the image of the invisible God, the first-born of all creation; for in him all things were created, in heaven and on earth, visible and invisible, whether thrones or dominions or principalities or authorities – all things were created through him and for him. He is before all things, and in him all things hold together. He is the head of the body, the Church; he is the beginning, the first-born from the dead, that in everything he might be pre-eminent. For in him all the fulness of God was pleased to dwell, and through him to reconcile to himself all things, whether on earth or in heaven, making peace by the blood of his cross (Col. 1:15–20).

Here Paul makes a threefold statement about the Lordship of Christ. *Everything* was made by and for Jesus Christ. *Everything* holds together in Jesus Christ. *Everything* will be reconciled by Jesus Christ. The everything that is reconciled is the same everything that was made. Things in heaven, things in earth, visible and invisible, dominions and authorities will be reconciled by the cross of Jesus Christ. Paul says that redemption is cosmic in scope, that God will restore what has been lost through sin, that through Jesus Christ humankind will take its rightful place in the creation and mould the world in love and obedience to God. We are God's 'workmanship, created in Christ Jesus for good works, which God prepared beforehand, that we should walk in Him' (Eph. 2:10). (See also John 3:16; 1 Cor. 5:19; Eph. 1:15–23; 3:8–11; Heb. 2:5–10).

The End of Times

The same theme is present when we look at the time to come in the closing acts of Scripture portrayed in the book of Revelation. John writes 'And I saw the holy city, new Jerusalem, coming out of heaven from God, prepared as a bride adorned for her husband' (Rev. 21:2). Here John portrays the culmination of redemption, the reconciliation of God with God's people, and even the outworking of the cultural mandate. What does John see? – no longer a garden, as in Paradise at the beginning, but a city, the creation of human culture. What had been begun in sin by Cain and at Babel is here portrayed in its perfection. It is true that this is *God's* city, but clearly it is God's *city*, not God's *garden*. John also sees the bride, not naked, as with Adam and Eve in paradise, but clothed, 'richly adorned for her husband'. Whereas Adam and Eve clothed themselves with fig leaves because of shame resulting from their sin, the appearance of the bride shows clothing perfected in and presented to Jesus Christ. John also sees that the kings of the earth will not only come into the city but 'shall bring their glory into it' (21:24). Human stewardship of the earth is perfected at the coming of Christ. The flow of human history, the outworking of God's act of creation, continues and is taken up in the creation of the new heavens and earth. 'The kingdom of the world has become the kingdom of our Lord and of his Christ . . .' (Rev. 11:15).

The 'cultural mandate' is revealed at the beginning and at the end of Scripture. It still tells us who we are, why God made us, and how we are to image God. It continues, is re-started, and is perfected in the redemptive work of Jesus Christ. It enters into the Kingdom of God. It is a gift of the Church to God as a testimony of obedience and as a fruition of God's command. The cultural mandate also tells us our task here, today, as a Church, as a called-out people, as the children of God. Redemption sets us on track once more.

CONCLUSION

Christian Service is as Wide as Creation

In the light of biblical teaching about creation, fall and redemption we can say with the Dutch theologian Herman Bavinck that 'Christianity stands before the soul in its truth and holiness only when we . . . glorify that Godlike work wherein the Father reconciles His created but fallen world through the death of His Son, and recreates it by His Spirit into a Kingdom of God.'[6]

The idea that God is at work saving the creation and that Christians are saved in order to take up their tasks in the world, in farming, building, manufacturing, technology, music, politics, family life, education, play and so on, may at first appear to be strange. Perhaps we are more used to hearing that God saves only souls, or that Christian faith concerns only or primarily 'spiritual' or personal matters, or that the Christian realm is confined to the church. But, while it is true that God saves souls and that the core of redemption is personal conversion, the scope of Christ's reconciliation and of Christian service is far wider. As Proverbs says 'For from the heart flows the spring of life' (4:23). A new heart must lead to a new life. A new life expresses itself throughout every part of God's world. God is not concerned with rescuing people from out of human existence, or only concerned with the internal life of believers, or only concerned with the internal relations of the Christian community itself. We must realise that God is concerned about politics, about architecture, about food and furniture, about poverty, suffering, about play, art and music, about neighbourhoods and economics, about animals and trees, about sex and intimacy, about the *reconciliation*, the healing from sin, *of all things* within the creation.

We must realise why, when Jesus begins his ministry at Nazareth, the first words that he quotes to describe what he is going to do are these:

> The Spirit of the Lord is upon me, because he has anointed me to preach good news to the poor. He has sent me to proclaim release to the captives, and recovering of sight to the blind, to set at liberty those who are oppressed, to proclaim the acceptable year of the Lord (Luke 4:18, 19).

These words certainly include those who are blind to faith, poor in spirit, and captive to sin. But they include far more. As James says 'Has not God chosen those who are poor in the world . . . ?' – clearly meaning those without money or status (James 2:5). Jesus announced that he would fight every kind of oppression and suffering and evil, that he would minister and create ministers for all the effects of sin throughout the creation.

Jesus' words of farewell in the 'Great Commission' echo the same theme. These words sometimes are read only as an exhortation to make individual converts. They certainly include that, but they also include far more. Jesus says 'Go therefore and make disciples of all nations, baptizing them in the name of the Father and of the Son and of the Holy Spirit, teaching them to observe all that I have commanded you; and lo, I am with you always, to the close of the age' (Matt. 28:18–20). Because he has authority in heaven and earth, the disciples must teach the *nations* to *observe all* he has commanded. The Great Commission itself includes all our tasks in the world.

Evangelism and Social Action

Often evangelicals who want to be socially responsible get confused about 'evangelism' and 'social responsibility'. Especially since the *Covenant* at the Lausanne Congress on World Evangelization (1974) expressed the conviction that evangelism and 'social concern' were equal but separate partners which together make up the mission of the Church, evangelical conferences have struggled to work out the relation between the two. One of the most recent conferences on the subject, involving the Lausanne Committee and the World Evangelical Fellowship in Grand Rapids in June 1982, remained 'ambiguous' and 'experienced difficulty in relating and integrating' evangelism and 'social responsibility'.[7]

Understanding Christian responsibility in God's world is hindered if we think of 'evangelism' and 'social responsibility' as two things which need to be added together to make up the whole Christian task. While it is not an 'either/or' option, neither is it a 'both/and' option, for this is not a very biblical way of getting at the problem. For one thing, the terms are too narrow. Evangelism includes winning individual converts, but it also includes proclaiming the whole *evangel*, God's good news for all creation. It includes proclamation to the nations about obedience to God, to the prisoners about freedom, to the poor about release – in short, it includes many of the things now labelled as 'social action'.

Repentance and conversion themselves involve turning from one life to another in every aspect of human existence.

'Social action' also covers a wide range of things. Its core meaning seems to be helping those in need, particularly those in physical need. But the whole range of service implied in Christ's redemptive activity cannot properly be captured by this term. Making music does not seem to be 'social action', nor is it 'evangelism', but God tells us to do it, and do it well. Making clothes and shoes and chairs that are good for people to use does not seem necessarily to be 'social action', but it is an essential part of the 'cultural mandate'. Similarly for composing, choreography, dance, plays, poems, growing crops and eating good food, teaching mathematics well, enjoying games, and writing this book. 'Social action' is too cramped a term for such a wealth of goals, service and achievement.

Adding 'social action' and 'evangelism' together still tends to portray them as separate things that must both be done, rather than as two facets of one overall task. In place of this two-fold scheme we should understand that our task is creation-wide and creation-deep. Our task as Christians is, in principle, to do everything in a Christian way that can be done by a human being – from what we eat when we get up in the morning (if we have anything to eat) to what clothes we put on, to how we get to work (if we have any work), to what we work at, making what, for how much, in what sort of conditions, to how we vote, how we engage in research, how we understand the news, how we relax, what we do with and for the poor, and so on throughout the livelong day. In all these activities we are called to be new creatures taking our place as the stewards of God's world, being servants of our neighbour and proclaimers of the good news of Jesus Christ. In all of them we are to learn what God calls us to do or, in other words, to see how redemption in Jesus Christ can bring healing and redirection. We are to proclaim and to show in our lives that Christ is Lord over every part of life. Just as every part of life is affected by human sin, so all parts of life can be renewed and redeemed by Jesus Christ. That is our only solid hope for families, factories or politics.

True Christian social action is always evangelistic work, for no area of life is 'neutral', supposedly immune from the effects of sin and the reach of redemption. We do not act merely on the basis of Christian 'principles' or 'morality', we are to act as witness to Jesus Christ. All areas of life must be linked to new life in Jesus Christ. In turn, true Christian evangelism is always social action because it lives and proclaims what is good news in each area of life.

Summary

Through the gospel God calls a new nation, a new people, a new humankind into being. As men and women turn to Jesus Christ in real, concrete, repentance from sin and, by grace through faith, are restored in God's favour, they begin to live out the healing and restoration of Christ's redemption and take up their Christian responsibility for the direction of human life and culture. Evangelism is, in a way, the recruiting process for this life whereby people come 'on board' for service to God's kingdom. Evangelism calls people to repentance and to a restored and renewed love for God and, through that love, to a new life of service to our neighbours. This is the Christian life. It is in terms of this life that we must understand our political tasks.

To carry out these political tasks we must understand the nature of politics as revealed through this biblical message of creation, fall and redemption. It is to this that we turn our attention in the next chapter.

3: Politics in God's World

THE BEGINNING OF JUDICIAL AUTHORITY

Cain

As Genesis recounts the development of human life in response to God throughout the first generations, it describes the development of the political order. In the story of Cain, in the 'generations of the heavens and the earth', we find the establishment of an authority for justice.[1] Cain murders his brother Abel and then the Lord appears saying 'The voice of your brother's blood is crying to me from the ground' (4:10).

The word translated as 'crying' or 'crying out' is *ze' aqah*. This is a word used frequently throughout the Old Testament for the cry, complaint or appeal of one who is suffering injustice. It is the word used to describe the cry of the poor and needy which resulted in the destruction of Sodom and Gomorrah (Gen. 18:20; Ezek. 16:49).[2] It is the cry of Israel in their slavery in Egypt (Exod. 2:23, 24). This word 'outcry' is also a technical legal term. It is an *appeal* to the courts to rectify injustice. When the court does not fulfil its duty then the outcry comes to the Lord who is the guardian of all justice. Thus, the appearance of God in defence of Abel is described in legal, in *political* terms. God appears as political authority.

In keeping with this role, God pronounces the sentence: 'now you are cursed from the ground . . . when you till the ground, it shall no longer yield you its strength; you shall be a fugitive and a wanderer on the earth' (Gen. 4:12). Cain explains that this is a greater punishment than he can bear and he describes his punishment as twofold: 'thou hast driven me this day away from the ground [i.e. to be a wanderer]; and from thy face shall I be hidden [to be a fugitive]' (v. 14). At this point the Lord says 'Not so!' But God is *not* saying that the punishment will be made easier, nor that Cain really doesn't deserve the punishment nor that Cain can't really bear the punishment. No, God is telling him that he has *misunderstood* the second part of what the punishment *actually is*. Whereas Cain thought he was being banished as a fugitive from the face of God (as well as a wanderer from the face of the ground), God corrects him and says this is not so.

When Cain complains that he will be hidden from God's face, his fear is actually that he will be denied God's judicial protection ('whoever finds me will kill me', v. 14). When the Scriptures speak of God 'hiding his face' they mean that God is not responding to the cry of the people, that God is hidden and does not come to Israel's just defence. In Ps. 27 the writer says that 'When evildoers assail me . . . I will inquire in his temple . . . Hear, O Lord, when I cry aloud, . . . Thou hast said, "Seek ye my face". My heart says to thee, "Thy face, Lord, do I seek". Hide not thy face from me. Turn not thy servant away in anger, thou who hast been my help. Cast me not off, forsake me not. . . .' [See also Ps. 10:11; 13:2; 22:25; 27:2, 4, 7, 8, 9; 30:8; 44:25; 69:18; 88:15; 102:3; 143:7; Job 13:2; Deut. 31:17, 18; 32:20, 35–36, 41ff; Isa. 8:17; Jer. 16:17; Mic. 3:4.] When God's face is revealed then righteousness prevails, when God's face is hidden then evil prospers and the wicked triumph. What Cain, as a murderer, is afraid of is not that he will have to keep hiding from God's face: his fear is exactly the opposite – it is that he *would be hidden* from God's face, that he would have no protector, that henceforth no righteousness or justice would be accorded him, that people could treat him as they liked. This is the awful doom against which Cain mistakenly complains.

It is to this part of Cain's complaint that God says 'not so!' God affirms that there will still be justice for Cain, that God's face will still be upon him. When Cain says 'whoever finds me will kill me', God, following legal formula, announces a law that 'if anyone slays Cain, vengeance shall be taken on him sevenfold'. (The 'sevenfold' here indicates 'rightly', 'justly' or 'completely', seven being a repeated Scriptural number for perfection or completeness.) God is not making the punishment easier, but is clarifying exactly what that punishment is. Contrary to what Cain thought, he is still under God's protection, he is still under God's order of justice, he is still before God's face. In saying this, God puts a mark on Cain in case anyone should try to kill him (v. 15). The 'mark of Cain' is not a curse like a brand that will always identify him as a murderer and an outcast. Rather it is a mark to *prevent* him from being killed, it is a mark that shows that God still *defends* Cain from lawlessness and will justly avenge his death. In fact the 'mark of Cain' is probably not a visual sign at all, it is more likely a 'verbal' sign, a word, a testimony given to Cain in the same way that God's verbal assurance to Moses was a 'sign' (Exod. 3:12). The sign was in fact the very words that the Lord spoke, the very assurance given to Cain that God's justice would be maintained.

In the story of Cain we see a legal order appearing. Penalties are established for Cain's murder of Abel but Cain in turn is not left to suffer anarchy. A legal order is established with penalties and this order incorporates Cain and anyone who seeks private revenge on him. The 'mark of Cain' is not merely particular to Cain as an individual: it is a sign that God has appointed an order to maintain justice.

After this confrontation with God, Cain goes away, marries, has children and founds a city. His generations are described briefly until we get to the story of his great, great, great grandson, Lamech. Lamech boasts 'I have slain a man for striking me . . . If Cain is avenged sevenfold, truly Lamech [is avenged] seventy-seven fold' (4:23, 24). Then, immediately, the narrative stops. We switch back to Adam and Eve and follow the line of another one of their sons, Seth. To Seth was born Enoch, and 'At that time men began to call on the name of the Lord' (v. 26).

A new line is introduced and the story of Lamech and his generations is broken off at the point at which it is apparent that the generations of Cain have issued in terrible sin. Lamech has refused to honour God's just order. Instead of giving a right, sevenfold response of justice according to God's order, Lamech has avenged a mere blow with death itself. With Lamech there is no justice, only revenge, a barbarism that strikes out in overkill at an enemy with no concern at all for just relationships. With Lamech humankind has forsaken its responsibility for justice, it has refused to heed the mark of Cain, God's just, legal order, and has substituted naked force and vengeance.

The story of Cain shows us that just as ploughing, hunting, city building and music-making appeared on the earth in the earliest generations, so also appeared a judicial, a legal order, what we would call now some sort of political order, separate from anarchy. Humankind has been given responsibility to maintain the just relations that God decrees. As history continues to unfold, a political authority appears and this authority is one which is to uphold justice, a 'seven-fold vengeance'.

Politics and Sin

Sometimes much is made of the fact that the political order appears after the fall and is first manifested in response to Cain's sin. Hence it is thought that government is not part of the original creation but is something which only comes into existence because of sin and will only last as long as sin does. This is a complex and vexed question. At this point we should just note that virtually all of the diversity of human actions and institutions are described in the Bible as coming after sin and as being affected by sin. This is true of, for example, music-making – which is also in the line of Cain (Gen. 4:21). But, while we may have our doubts about what comes over the radio these days, it is doubtful that we can say that music only exists because of sin! It depends on the song sung (Rev. 14:2, 3). Similarly, the use of bricks and tar is first described as part of the building of the tower of Babel, a project conceived in sin (Gen. 11:3–5).

Because of these other examples, we cannot conclude from the story of Cain that politics and law are only necessary because of sin. An answer to this question will depend on whether we see the state, and the justice associated with it, as having only a *negative* task (i.e. the restraint of sin) or whether we see it also as having a *positive* task in the *promotion* of justice between people. Such a positive task can be rooted in the way God has made the world and would continue to be part of humankind's cultural mandate even after sin has been kept away. The fact that the book of Revelation says that kings will bring their glory and the honour of the nations into the New Jerusalem suggests that the political enterprise has its own intrinsic merit apart from the effects of sin (Rev. 21:24–26).

What we can say on the basis of the story of Cain is that the institution of law has an intrinsic connection with justice. Law is to uphold the right relations that God calls people to have with one another. It is to provide a response that is sevenfold – one which is right, fitting and complete.

THE EVOLUTION OF POLITICAL INSTITUTIONS

After the story of Cain and of Noah, we find the history of Abraham. Here the Bible focusses on the people that God has chosen and will train to be the bearers of the Messiah who will redeem the whole earth. God still intervenes directly for the maintenance of justice, as with Sodom and Gomorrah (Gen. 18:20; Ezek. 16:49), and with the Egyptian's lust after Sarah (Gen. 12:17). But increasingly we find more human activity to do with maintaining a just order.

Abraham, as the father of a family which is by this point a clan or a mini-tribe, functions as the family law maker and rule giver. In Abraham parental and political authority are combined. When he divides up the land between himself and his nephew, Lot, he appears to be exercising both offices (Gen. 13:2–12). Later, when he rescues Lot from the warring kings, he refuses to take any booty but only what is rightfully owing him (14:13–16, 21–24). Abraham does not take what he can get away with but instead maintains a just response to violence for which he is praised by the 'priest of God Most High', Melchizedek (14:18–20). Later, 'The Lord says "Shall I hide from Abraham what I am about to do? . . . No, for I have chosen him that he may charge his children and his household after him to keep the way of the Lord by doing righteousness and justice . . ." ' (18:17–19). God reveals that Abraham has been chosen to maintain and continue the doing of justice throughout the generations. Because of Abraham's task, God decides to tell him that Sodom and Gomorrah are to be destroyed.

Abraham's response to God shows that he was beginning to appreciate and apply the implications of God's just order for the world. Abraham actually begins to argue with God about it: 'Wilt thou indeed destroy the righteous with the wicked . . . suppose there are fifty righteous . . . ? Far be it from thee to do such a thing, to slay the righteous with the wicked, so that the righteous fare as the wicked! Far be that from thee! Shall not the judge of all the earth do right?' (18:23–25). Abraham has seen what justice is about. He declares that God is the judge of *all* the earth, that God's order of justice, God's requirement of justice continues and is extended to all humankind, even to those outside the chosen people, even to those in Sodom and Gomorrah. Abraham points out that one cannot treat the righteous and the wicked in the same way, but that they must be rewarded rightly ('do right') according to their deeds. He presses the point home – 'what if there are forty five [righteous in the city]? or forty? . . . or ten?' (18:26–32). In the end God yields to Abraham's call for justice and decides not to punish the cities if there are ten righteous people left in them. In Abraham we see a true judicial office, a judging of people rightly, an administering of punishment and reward according to what God has commanded. Abraham has taken up the task of God's authority upon earth, even questioning God on the basis of God's own promises and commitments. He fulfils his calling as one truly made in the image of God by moulding history as he wrestles with God!

For a while this political and parental authority remain intertwined, but then God calls out Moses as one chosen to respond to the ze'aqah, the outcry for justice of Israel in Egypt (Exod. 3:7, 10). In response to God's call, Moses goes into Egypt and eventually delivers Israel out of captivity. He leads them through the wilderness and tells the Israelites of God's law for their lives, how they are to live together in the new land to which they shall come. In Moses, parental and political authority have become distinct.

At Sinai God announces the Law, the revelation of a just order for the patterning of Israel's life together as persons, as families, as a nation. In turn Israel covenants to love God and keep the commandments. Moses announces the laws concerning marriage, adultery, stealing, murder, manslaughter, debt, land ownership, house ownership, legal testimony, dealing with foreigners, and so on through all the types of relationships which will exist in the nation. He then calls the *elders* of the people to witness the law and, where necessary, to carry out its decisions and consequences.

Later, when Israel has settled in the promised land and has done evil and been plundered by its enemies, 'Then the Lord raised up *judges*, who saved them out of the power of those who plundered them' (Judg. 2:16). Just as with the prophets, so we read that 'the Spirit of the Lord came upon' the Judges (Judg. 3:10; 6:34; 11:29; compare Isa. 42:1; 54:21). Unlike Moses the judges appear to be distinct from the priests. In the book of Judges we find a growing, but certainly not complete, distinction of parental, priestly and political authority. Certainly, as the judges now include great women of faith such as Deborah (chs 4, 5), political authority is not paternal, patriarchal authority. There are now diverse authorities, of parent, priest and judge, each responsible to God for a specific task (2 Chr. 26:18).

Later in the book of Judges (8:27ff; 9:1ff) and in Samuel (1 Sam. 8) we read how Israel seeks to pervert political authority by putting a king in the place of the judges, a king who would exercise authority in place of God. Gideon resisted this call (Judg. 8:23) but Abimelech, after murdering his brothers, gets himself proclaimed king. Abimelech then initiates a reign of violence and slaughter (Judg. 9) until God makes his evil recoil on his own head (9:56).

In the time of Samuel the people once again call for a king. They have two reasons for doing so. One was that Samuel's sons were perverting justice (1 Sam. 8:3) and the other was that Israel wanted to 'be like all the nations'. Samuel warns them of dire consequences (8:11–18), but God tells him to 'hearken to their voice and make them a king' (8:22).

Israel wanted a king partly for wrong motives, to make war, to imitate the nations about them. But God goes along anyway, saying that the king 'shall save my people from the hand of the Philistines, for I have seen the affliction of my people, because their cry has come to me' (9:16). Despite Israel's wrong motives and their desire to put a king in God's place (8:7–9; 10:19), God still appoints a king as an action of restoration and justice. Perhaps Samuel's fatherly eyes could not see the injustice that his sons the judges were doing, so that God has to step in.

Samuel then tells the people of the rights and duties of kingship and writes them down in a book (10:25). The first king, Saul, in turn starts off his kingship by abiding by the ordinances of God (11:12–15), so Samuel announces: 'behold, the LORD has set a king over you . . . and if both you and the king who reigns over you will follow the Lord your God, it will be well' (12:13, 14). The king becomes the anointed of the Lord (26:8–12) and later, Solomon, king of Israel, is also known as Jedidiah, the 'beloved of Yahweh' (2 Sam. 12:24, 25). Thus the institution of kingship arrives in Israel. Although Israel desired it wrongfully, the Lord graciously provides it and makes it a source of blessing and justice.

There is now some doubt about what the king was actually supposed to do. He certainly was to lead in battle, but beyond that things are confused. He did not make laws, for these had already been given at Sinai. He may have acted as a judge, but the elders and judges still continued and carried out that function.[3] Later still the prophets evolved from out of the seers (1 Sam. 9:9). The prophets took up the role of challenging the kings and judges, and of calling them not to pervert righteousness but to uphold the just order of Yahweh.

This, then, is the evolution of political authority in God's people, Israel. This office is not that of the priest, nor the prophet, nor the parent, nor the father: it is a distinct authority under the Lord. We see the gradual development of distinct political offices, of people who have authority from the Lord to judge justly, to reward both the righteous and the unrighteous according to their deeds.

THE ROLE OF GOVERNMENT

Political Authority

The teaching about politics in the New Testament follows in the path of that in the Old Testament. After declaring that all the creation will share in the redemption of Jesus Christ and during the course of showing the Roman Christians how then they should live, Paul tells his readers that government, even the pagan government of the Roman Empire, is neither a demonic thing nor a realm apart from the ordinances of God. He tells them 'there is no authority except from God, and those that exist have been instituted by God'. He reiterates that the political authority 'is God's servant for your good' (Romans 13:1, 4). Jesus echoes the same theme in telling Pilate: 'You would have no power over me unless it had been given you from above' (John 19:11). Peter says 'Be subject for the Lord's sake to every human institution, whether it be to the emperor . . . or to governors' (1 Pet. 2:13, 14).

Political authority is authority from God. Those who hold political office, even if they are unbelievers, can do so because God has authorised such an office for the governing and service of humankind. Political authority is not an area apart from the gospel, but can be an area of ministry performed by ministers of God. It can be ministry just as much as any office in the church. This authority is not a thing separate from the reign of Jesus Christ but is itself a manifestation of the authority of the 'King of Kings' (Rev. 1:5, 17:14; 19:16) who said 'All authority in heaven and earth is given unto me' (Matt. 28:18).

Paul shows that government, in its proper task, has an authority under and from God that individual people do not have. In the Sermon on the Mount Jesus tells the disciples: 'Do not resist one who is evil. But if anyone strikes you on the right cheek, turn to him the other also' (Matt. 5:39) and 'Judge not, that you be not judged' (Matt. 7:1). Paul reiterates this teaching in his letter to the Romans: 'Beloved, never avenge yourselves, but leave it to the wrath of God; for it is written, "Vengeance is mine, I will repay says the Lord" ' (Romans 12:19–21). Then, immediately after he has echoed Jesus' admonition against revenge, Paul goes on to describe the task of government. He says governments are 'instituted by God . . . [he] who is in authority is the servant of God to execute his wrath on the wrongdoer' (13:1, 4).

Paul's point is quite clear. It is God, not we ourselves who will punish evil and reward good. God's means of doing so, or at least one of God's means of doing so, is the governing authorities which God has provided to exercise precisely that role. Leaving it to God to execute justice also means leaving it to the governing authorities to execute justice. No individual person has the personal right of revenging evil, nor can they give that right to another.[4] But because God, in the course of human history, provides governments with particular authority to execute justice, then those who rightfully hold government authority may and should avenge evil and reward good.

Because of Paul's distinction between personal action and authorised political action, it is not right to counterpose the Sermon on the Mount to Romans 13. It is not right to say that Jesus' reign is one of nonviolence and peace as opposed to the reign of government where force may be necessary. Governments are also under the reign of Jesus Christ and, under that reign, they have the particular task of avenging good and evil. Nor is it right to say that while it may indeed be true that governments derive their authority from God yet they do so only under a separate dispensation, such as 'God's order of preservation', distinct from 'God's order of redemption' which is supposedly manifested only in the church. *The state is what God through Jesus Christ has set up to maintain justice.* Its officers are as much ministers of God as are prophets and priests. The authority of the state is not some sort of separate authority outside of Christ and redemption. It is authority from Jesus Christ to whom *all* authority is given just as much as is authority in the church. 'Thrones or dominions or principalities or authorities – all things were created through him and for him . . . in him all things hold together' (Col. 1:16–17). The gospel itself has its place in political power (1 Pet. 3:22).

Because political authority is an aspect of the authority of Jesus Christ, the first thing that Paul tells the Roman Christians to do is to submit to that authority. This submission is not only to avoid 'wrath' but is 'also for the sake of conscience,' (13:5) – such submission is right and proper. Furthermore 'he who resists the authorities resists what God has appointed and . . . will incur judgment' (13:3). It is plain that submitting to government authority is not an optional thing for a Christian, or for anyone. Government is not a happenstance thing, something to be followed only in so far as we approve of its policies. We cannot claim that as we are followers of Christ then we are obedient only to his and not to the government's authority, for government authority is one aspect of Christ's authority. The Christian realm is not one apart from the governmental realm, for to obey governments is one part of obeying God.

The Specific Task of Government

Although we can outline the authority, task and place of political institutions in such sweeping terms, we must not become mesmerised by them. Governments must not be thought of as mini-gods that can do anything while our only responsibility is passively just to obey. That this is clearly *not* the case is shown by the fact that in each instance where the New Testament speaks of governing authorities it describes them in terms of the specific task they have to do, in terms of what they been given their specific authority *for*.

Peter writes of 'governors . . . sent by him to punish those who do wrong and to praise those who do right' (1 Pet. 2:14). Paul writes that 'rulers are not a terror to good conduct, but to bad . . . he is the servant of God to execute his wrath on the wrong-doer' (Romans 13:3, 4). As Paul knew that actually existing governments *do* in fact punish those who do good, Jesus Christ being the prime example (1 Cor. 2:7, 8), then what he writes is clearly indicating what the *proper* task of governments is. Governments have *a particular task* and authority. They do not have authority to do anything they might please. Jesus said 'Render to Caesar the things that are Caesar's, and to God the things that are God's' (Mark 12:17; see also Acts 5:29). Clearly then Caesar cannot claim *all* things. In fact, as we have seen, Caesar's authority can only come from God and is, in turn, defined by God. God and Caesar are not two separate realms. Caesar is *under* God and, hence, should be rendered only what God says should be rendered – that is, obedience and honour according to Caesar's rightful task.

Nor should we think that in Romans 13 Paul gives government *carte blanche* in its activities. He does not blandly accept the *status quo* of Roman Imperialism and advocate only a quiescent submission to it. Although Romans 13 has often been interpreted, as it was by Christians in Nazi Germany, as a call to total and unconditional obedience to whatever government might have happened to get into power, in fact the epistle shows just the opposite. Paul's statements are anything but conservative. Paul knows that Jesus said that His own kingship was not like the kingdoms of this world (John 18:36).[5] The vital power that Jesus brings into the world to transform it, 'to bring to nothing the things that are' (1 Cor. 1:28), to 'put down the mighty from their thrones, and exalt those of low degree' (Luke 1:52), is a power that will not bow before petty human tyrannies but will challenge and transform them. Paul himself, as a servant of Jesus, was frequently in prison and in trouble with political authorities.

What Paul writes in Romans 13 is a re-interpretation in the light of the gospel of the then accepted political order. Paul flies in the face of the self-image of the Empire. He criticises its legal structure and downgrades its claimed political authority. Paul says that governments are servants, a quite remarkable thing to say. In the light of the gospel, governments are not lords, they do not exist for themselves, they are not the supreme authority. In a time when the Emperors were beginning to set themselves up as deities, Paul says no!, they are servants. In saying this Paul is showing that, whatever the Emperors might claim, the state cannot define itself, it is not the source of all authority. At bottom, he is saying that the Empire is not sovereign. This is why Paul can conclude his discussion of politics in Romans 13 by saying 'Pay all of them their dues, taxes to whom taxes are due, revenue to whom revenue is due . . .' (13:7ff). Give them what is *due* to them, what is owing them, what is *right for them* to have. The order of justice determines the relation of ruler and subject, government and citizen, and delineates their place in relation to one another. We do not surrender all to government, rather we give what is *due* to it. Paul relativises the Roman Imperial order. He refuses to accept the Emperor's ultimate authority and says that the Emperor is *under* God, a servant, one with a particular task to do and who may not stray from that task.

Jesus and Political Authority

It seems to be the case that, as far as the Roman authorities were concerned, Jesus was crucified for doing just what Paul says in Romans 13. When the priests at his trial interrogated Jesus they concentrated on his claim to be the Messiah, the Christ (Matt. 26:61–64; Mark 14:60; Luke 22:66–71), but when they brought him before Pilate they took a more directly political tack. They said to the Roman governor: 'We found this man perverting our nation and forbidding us to give tribute to Caesar, and saying that he himself is Christ a king' (Luke 23:2). This is the line of questioning that Pilate pursued and he asked: 'Are you the King of the Jews?' (Matt. 27:11; Mark 15:2, 8, 12; Luke 23:3). The Roman soldiers mocked Jesus with the words 'Hail, King of the Jews!' (Matt. 27:29; Luke 23:37) but the people cried 'let him save himself, if he is the Christ of God, his Chosen One' (Luke 23:35; but not always, see Matt. 27:41, 42). The Roman inscription on the cross was 'This is the King of the Jews'.

The priests knew the Romans would be worried about someone claiming to be a king and so this was the charge they mentioned to Pilate. This was indeed what the Romans concentrated on. We should not delude ourselves with the idea that because Jesus' kingship was of a different type than worldly kingdoms, that therefore it was a thing unconnected to the kingships of the earth. While Jesus' kingship certainly does not *derive from* or come out *of* this world order and while its marks are radically different from the then existing political orders (Luke 27:24–27; Acts 1:6; Romans 14:17), yet his kingship has every implication for who the kings of the world are and what they do. The Romans were far more politically astute than modern Christians who read through Luke's description of Jesus' passion as though it were politically irrelevant. The Romans were representatives of a political order that claimed to be *the* authority, the *final* authority. They believed that all other authorities were *under* the Emperor. They would not accept any other allegiance which could be higher than or could countermand their own authority. The Romans knew all about the political meaning of religion and knew that when Jesus said that he was a king (Matt. 21:5; John 1:49–51) he was already involved in a conflict with the political order. It didn't really matter what type of king Jesus said he was for, even though Jesus was not about to take political power (Acts 1:6–8), his life, death and resurrection would make sure that political power could never be the same again.

Jesus proclaimed himself as an authority *above* kings. He proclaimed that earthly power could only derive from himself (John 19:11). Jesus' life and teaching and messiahship showed that the Emperor was not ultimate, but subordinate. While the followers of Jesus would willingly obey the authorities as ministers of God, they could never yield total allegiance to the Empire, or to any other political order. They had another allegiance, one which could conflict with and override their duty to the Emperor. As long as they were faithful to God they could never be taken for granted, for their allegiance to God was an overriding force which relativised their allegiance to the Emperor. Faithful Christians, while knowing and obeying political authorities as ministers of the Lord, should never be easy subjects; they must always judge political authority in terms of God's superior authority.

We should not be confused by the conservatism of Christians in recent years into thinking that Christians *have* been easy subjects. In fact the history of the church has invariably been one of questioning, challenging and redefining the political order. The dividedness of Christian allegiance has been a constant source of complaint for western political theorists such as Machiavelli, Hobbes or Rousseau, who wished to make the state the encompassing community. In fact, rather than due to any specific Christian *teaching*, it was probably the mere continued *existence* of the church, as a body separate from the political order, that kept alive the idea of limits on state power and provided the base for the growth of modern constitutional government.

But Jesus and Paul say more than merely that governments are servants. Paul says that they are 'God's servants *for your good*' (Romans 13:4). Jesus says something similar, 'The kings of the gentiles exercise lordship over them . . . But not so with you, rather let the greatest among you become as the youngest, and the leader as one who serves. . . . I am among you as one who serves' (Luke 22:25–27). This is the core of the gospel message for politics – that *political authority exists for the good of the citizenry*, that political power is to be understood as servanthood, that government is called under God to minister and administer justice for the benefit of all people and to defend those who are oppressed.

JUSTICE

Justice as what is 'Due'

We have seen that political authority is concerned with the administration of *Justice*. God is just (Deut. 32:4), in fact all God's ways are just (Ps. 89:14; 96:13). Jeremiah describes Jesus Christ as 'the Lord is our righteousness [i.e. justice]' (Jeremiah 23:6). Isaiah says 'he shall judge the poor, and decide with equity for the meek of the earth' (Isa. 11:4), 'He will bring forth justice to the nations' (Isa. 42:1). Justice is one of the things that God requires between people and, in turn, Jesus is the bringer of justice. Justice is an inherent and central element of the gospel. The restoration of genuine human community in terms of the covenant between God and humankind necessarily implies justice and a politics founded in justice.

This justice is to be mediated through political authority. As the Psalmist says: 'Give the king thy justice, O God, and thy justice to the royal son . . . May he defend the cause of the poor of the people, give deliverance to the needy, and crush the oppressor' (Ps. 72:1–4; see also Ps. 45:4–8).

But what is meant by 'justice'? Like any important word its meaning is much easier to sense than to define. In fact justice is almost impossible to define. However, we can get some idea from the Scriptures of what it means. The Psalm from which we have just quoted ties justice in with the defence of the poor, the needy and the oppressed and, in turn, with the punishment of the oppressor. This same sense is clear in the New Testament where the repeated theme of politics is rewarding the righteous and punishing the evildoer. In fact we might better describe politics in terms of *rewarding both* the righteous and the evildoer, but *rewarding* them, paying them back, according to their deeds. Evil deeds bring evil consequences, good deeds bring good consequences.

The examples to which we referred earlier bring out further senses of justice. With Cain we read of 'sevenfold' vengeance, which contains the sense of what is 'fitting' or 'complete', a full but not an overfull vengeance (Gen. 4:15). Abraham's argument with God that 'shall not the judge of all the earth do right [i.e. justly]' (Gen. 18:25), and that the righteous could not be slain with the wicked (18:24), shows that justice requires responses that fit with the actual culpability of those involved.

This theme is repeated when the law is given to Israel at Sinai. God pronounces the famous '*lex talionis*': 'you shall give life for life, eye for eye, tooth for tooth, hand for hand, foot for foot, burn for burn, wound for wound, stripe for stripe' (Exod. 21:24, 25). This saying is often pictured as a brutal and barbaric one, replete with images of merciless blood feuds and of eyes being plucked out. But the '*lex talionis*' is nothing of the kind. Nowhere in all the laws of Israel are these types of punishment advocated. We simply do not find eye-plucking or foot-chopping. The immediate context of this saying shows it has a particular type of message to give about justice. The very next verse says: 'When a man strikes the eye of his slave, male or female, and destroys it, he shall let the slave go free, for the eye's sake' (v. 26). If we were to interpret an eye for an eye literally then the next verse would be a complete contradiction, for the slave does not pluck out the master's eye but instead goes free. However, this next verse and the ones that follow are not contradictions of but are *applications* of 'an eye for an eye'. The example of the slave is an *illustration* of the principle that has been announced.

The point of 'an eye for an eye' is that you can't respond to an offence against you by taking *two* eyes, or *two* teeth, or *two* lives. The severity of the punishment has to fit the severity of the crime, whether that be great or small. Smaller misdeeds deserve smaller responses, larger misdeeds deserve larger responses. In short, 'an eye for an eye' illustrates the judicial principle of *equity* – treat equal cases alike and let the measure of reward or punishment be appropriate to the gravity of the deed. This principle of law given at Sinai gives a clearer sense of what the original 'sevenfold vengeance' of Cain is all about. This broad sense of justice is quite similar to the classical definitions about 'giving each their due'.

Aspects of Justice

Once we go beyond these general statements about justice and inquire as to exactly what *is* due to people then things become more difficult. The hebrew words meaning justice, which unfortunately are usually translated in our English Bibles as 'righteousness', occur in various forms more than 500 times in the Old Testament. The corresponding New Testament sets of terms occur more than 200 times.[6] Many of these different instances involve subtle and complex variations on the major theme. Consequently we can only give a very brief summary of the various facets of justice.

However, before doing this, we should pause to realise just *how much* of the Bible is about justice. The word 'righteousness', which we often use instead, seems to have different connotations in the modern world and is often used by Christians to mean 'holiness' or 'morality'. However, if we substitute, as we should, variations of the term 'justice' wherever we read 'righteousness', then the Bible begins to sound quite different. We realise that *justice* appears and is stressed again and again throughout the Scriptures in reference to God, to Jesus Christ, to kings, judges, priests, prophets, the poor and the rich. Yet, despite this overflowing of justice, we often pass over these texts without noticing, much less heeding, their implications. For example, evangelicals have engaged in mammoth speculations about the eschatological meaning of the more obscure parts of Daniel, often without paying attention to the teaching in the book about what the nations are and how God is calling them to behave. We must stop and realise that the Bible is a book full to overflowing with commands to do justice.

Justice refers, first of all, not to persons or acts but to the fact that there can be a just ordering of things according to God's will. God maintains a just order in the creation. We are to conform our actions to this order and we are to judge all things and all actions in terms of this order. When we say that something is just or unjust we are measuring it in terms of God's requirement for justice. This just order should be upheld by people but, if they do not act justly, God still upholds justice in the world. God is just and judges in a right way. One aspect of this justice is that God shows no partiality and is not a respecter of persons. This means that all people are judged equally before God (John 5:3; 7:24; Acts 17:31; Romans 2:11; Eph. 6:9; 1 Pet. 1:17; 2:23; Rev. 16:7; 19:2).

Because God requires all things to be just then justice is a standard which can be applied not only to people. Even weights and measures must be just, i.e. they must be fair, they must represent what they are supposed to represent (Lev. 19:36; Deut. 25:18). Wages must be just, political arrangements must be just.

All people must be just in the sense that they must act justly in relation to others. Being just, in this sense, means that we must refrain from such things as idolatry, adultery, robbery and violence. Such justice requires not only abstaining from negative things but also actually pursuing positive things. The just person must care for those who are hungry and naked, defend the poor, and judge fairly between others (cf. Ezek. 18:5–9). The 'unjust' are the ones who do not do these things. In the Old and the New

Testaments various people are described as just in this way (Matt. 5:45; Luke 1:6; 15:7; 23:50; Acts 24:15).

Even though, in absolute terms, nobody is just (Romans 3:10) because we have all fallen short of what God requires of us, nevertheless people can also be described as just when, by the grace of God, they are in a right relation with God. Hence through the gospel we are made just, not in the sense that we are personally perfect, but in the sense that through the death of Jesus Christ, our sins are forgiven and we can enter into a just relationship with God: 'he condemned sin in the flesh in order that the just requirement of the law might be fulfilled in us' (Romans 8:3–4).

In court cases people can also be judged as 'just' or 'unjust'. In a legal conflict between two people the judge will pronounce one of them as the just one. This does not mean that this person is without sin but that *in this particular case* this person is in the right. When a person is just in this sense, this means that the judge has found in their favour. For example, in a conflict over land between two people the judge will decide who is 'in the right' in the case and this person is then called 'just' and given the right to the land.

Judges must themselves be just. They are the ones who decide who is just, who is in the right, in a particular case and when they do so properly then they are called 'just' judges. An unjust judge is one who does not judge rightly. A judge is unjust if he or she takes bribes or shows partiality to one party, or kowtows to the rich and does not defend the poor (Deut. 16:18ff; 25:1).[7] In this respect judges are to be imitators of God, showing no partiality but judging rightly just as God shows no partiality and judges rightly. This is part of what it means that judges take up a God-given task – in the matter of judgement they must do what God would do. This is why governments are described as ministers of God.

Kings are also to act like judges. They are to be just in deciding who is just and unjust. In the Old Testament, as kings did not usually handle court cases, their major just task was to protect the poor and needy from exploitation (see Chapter 5E).

God's order of justice which encompasses people, things, relations, judges and kings should not be thought of as a static thing, a sort of frozen neo-Platonic Idea. Justice requires new actions as new historical circumstances arise. It does not specify a given type of social order but is always a means of evaluating whatever types of social order we shape. Nor should justice be equated with legalism: it is not a simple totting up of legal precedent or an application of abstract legal principles. Justice is a drive to *make* things right, it is a movement toward good and lifegiving relationships. Justice must always include *kindness* (Matt. 25:31ff) and *generosity* (2 Cor. 9:9ff).

What is 'Due' to God's Creatures?

Overall, the sense of justice conveyed by and elaborated in the Scriptures is that there is an order of right relations between God, persons and things. This is an order of justice. Patterns of relations which conform to this order are just ones. Human beings are called to conform to this order in all their doings and, insofar as they do so, then they may be described as just and their actions may be described as just. To deal with someone or something justly means to give them or it its 'due', its rightful place within God's order of creation.

Of course this understanding of justice immediately raises the question of what *is due* to the differing creatures in God's world. There are many answers offered to this question in the modern world. Some say that people should get what they deserve, others say that it should be what they have worked for, or the same amount as everybody else, or the same opportunity as everybody else, or whatever it is they need. Even if we focus on 'need', we have to face the question of 'need in order to do what?'

A Christian answer to the question of what is due to people or anything else must be answered in terms of the place of everything in God's creation. Everyone in the world is responsible to God in their particular place. Each of us has tasks to do and responsibilities to take up. Each of us has a 'calling' or 'callings' to fulfil. We must be faithful husbands or wives, loving and wise parents, industrious and careful workers, caring neighbours, responsible citizens, steadfast friends. What is due to us is related to the callings we have. We can say that due to each of us is what we need in order to discharge our life's responsibilities. If we put this in more modern language we can say that each of us has a right to fulfil the callings that God has given us.

Hence justice means comparing the place, the callings, of everything in God's creation and making sure that they have what they need (whether that be freedom or protection or goods and services) relative to others. Emil Brunner's summary of this is useful:

> The Christian conception of justice . . . is determined by the conception of God's order of creation. What corresponds to the Creator's ordinance is just – to that ordinance which bestows on every creature (i.e. created thing), with its being, the law of its being, and its relationship to other creatures. The 'primal order' to which everyone refers in using the words 'just' or

'unjust', the 'due' which is rendered to each, is the order of creation, which is the will of the creator made manifest.[8]

The biblical teaching of justice bears witness to the biblical teaching on creation. Being just requires giving something its right, its created place in God's world. The doing of such justice is, in the Scriptures, related to the task of political authorities. These authorities are to judge, impartially and without favour, the relations of things in the creation in terms of justice and injustice. They are to rectify that which is unjust by restoring things to their right relation. This restoration implies, and is itself, a rewarding of those who are just (or on the just side of the relation) and a punishing (or the negative rewarding) of those who are on the unjust side of the relation.

THE LIMITS ON GOVERNMENT

The mandate given to political authorities is to do justice. But this is not a task given *only* to political office bearers, for *all* people are supposed to do justly in *all* their doings (cf. Ps. 15:1ff; Ezek. 18:5–9: Luke 1:6; James 5:16). Even measuring bowls are supposed to be just. Hence justice alone is not enough to define the government's role. In order to understand what governments are supposed to do, we must say more than that they are to do justice. We have to know how governments' mandate to justice is different from that of people at large. We have to know the particular circumstances in which governments are to act.

One thing which is different about governments is, as we have seen, that they have the authority to punish evil and to reward good, they have the power of the 'sword', they alone can legitimately use *force*. But more than this must be said in order to specify *when* governments should use this authority and power. This point is especially important because governments don't have the authority to do just anything that they might feel like. It is vitally important that they be kept in their proper place for in the Scriptures there is a repeated refrain concerning the dangers of overpowerful and overreaching government authority. The litany of injustices and disasters that Samuel tells Israel would follow on from their having a king (1 Sam. 8:11–18) is amply illustrated by the actions of most of the kings that they actually had. When the book of Revelation pictures the coming together of the forces of evil in the world, it does so in terms of a beast portrayed like a political authority – 'Who is like the beast, and who can fight against it? . . . And authority was given it over every tribe and people and tongue and nation' (Rev. 13:4, 7).

With utter realism the Bible portrays governments as both potentially and actually dangerous and as easily perverted. Governments in this fallen world wield tremendous power, the power of the sword, the power to force and coerce. Therefore we must be doubly careful to ensure that this particular servant of God *remains* a servant and does not become a lord or a tyrant. We must know not only what governments are supposed to do but also what they are *not* supposed to do.

We have seen already that God gave authority to priests (the Levites) and prophets as well as to elders, judges and kings. Each of these offices manifests a particular form of God-given authority. Each of these has a particular type of service for which they have authority and responsibility from God. God's authority on earth is not centred in any one type of person or in any one type of institution, be that government or anything else. There are many areas of authority, such as those of husband, wife, parents, employers, bishops and deacons (Eph. 5:21–6:9; Col. 3:18–4:5; 1 Tim. 3). The laws of Israel also were not all of a juridical, political kind. The tenth commandment is 'Thou shalt not covet' which seems to be a command not capable of any legal enforcement. In fact the basic command to love the Lord your God completely defies any political enforcement whatsoever. It is literally impossible to *compel* anybody to obey this commandment. Israel's political authorities were not given the responsibility to enforce all the law. Other authorities had their own place and task.

We each are responsible to God in distinct ways. There is no one body or person on earth who represents *all* of God's authority. Responsibility and authority are not channelled through one single institution. Neither the Emperor, nor the apostle, nor the master, nor the teacher, nor the parent, nor the husband nor wife, can claim to be the only or the ultimate authority. One of these cannot override another in the others' proper sphere of authority. Each and all have the responsibility, and the authority that goes with it, to do a particular task within the creation.

This same point is emphasised by the analogies which recur in the New Testament to Christians as parts of the human body. After Paul has told his readers not to be conformed to the world he tells them to have a 'sober judgement' about their roles and abilities, and says:

> For as in one body we have many members, and all the members do not have the same function, so we, though many, are one body in Christ and individually members of one another. Having gifts that differ according to the grace given to us, let us use them; if prophecy, in proportion to our faith; if service in our

serving; he who teaches, in his teaching; he who exhorts, in his exhortation; he who contributes, in liberality; he who gives aid, with zeal; he who does acts of mercy, with cheerfulness (Romans 12:4–8; see also 1 Cor. 12:12–31; Eph. 4:4–16).

Paul has the local church immediately in mind when he writes this but that should not deter us from seeing its wider implications. All of the world is Christ's and the church is to fill that world and all of its offices with renewing life. The body of Christ is also a model for the world because in him *all* things hold together (Col. 1:17).

All of this means that we should not think of politics as everything or the most important thing. C. S. Lewis once wrote that Christians make two mistakes about evil spirits: one was to ignore or dismiss them, the other was to be totally fascinated by them. Politics is similar in this respect. We must ensure that we do not make either of these mistakes. To try to make politics the centre of life is as bad as trying to ignore it entirely. The political order is only one sphere of responsibility before God. Christ alone has all authority. The political order has a particular authority for particular things and it should not try to go beyond those bounds. Merely because something is a problem, even a problem of justice, this does not mean that the political authorities can or should try to solve it.

We can delineate part of government's authority by realising that it should not override other authorities such as those of the church, the parent, or the individual person. The authority of government ends where the authorities of others begin. In fact we can say more because, unlike the family or the church, the government is not given any specific zone within the creation where it is to act. Yet, at the same time, government is charged with the responsibility for maintaining an overall order of justice. In the light of these two things, taken together, we may say that the governing authority's task is to *justly interrelate* the authorities, the areas of responsibility, of others within the creation. Government is not to supplant other authorities but it is to make sure that relations, such as those between person and person, between family and family, between church and church or church and state, are ones which conform to God's requirements for a just order.

GOVERNMENT AND PEOPLE

Representation

Jesus teaches us that the first is the last. He teaches us that authority is not lording it over one another but is servanthood (Matt. 20:8, 27; Mark 9:35). This theme is reiterated throughout the New Testament: *authority is servanthood*. To have authority from God is to have the right and responsibility to serve your neighbours in a particular way (Romans 1:14; 13:4; 1 Cor. 3:15; 9:19; 1 Pet. 1:12; 2:16). Governments are not called to be absolute but are called to be servants. They are not called to be self-centred powers but rather servants for the good of the citizenry. Nor are governments to be alien, foreign things, which stand over and apart from the population. This can be seen if we study the development of governmental authority through the Bible.

Clearly the Bible does not speak directly about such modern conceptions as 'democracy', 'elections', or 'representative government'. But that should not deter us from seeking to understand these things in the light of the Bible. Throughout the Scriptures we read of such matters as office, responsibility and covenant, and these are matters which are fundamental to understanding the relation of governments and populations.[9] In the story of Israel, we find instances of people who can be regarded, in a general way, as political representatives. The history of Israel is replete with mentions of the role of elders. These elders are variously described as 'princes', 'foremen', 'heads', and 'leaders' (Exod. 5:6, 15, 19; 19:7; Num. 1:16; 1 Chr. 29:6; Hos. 5:10). They derived their authority from God and were often appointed by such people as Moses or Samuel. But, at the same time, they were also clearly *chosen* by the people of Israel as their *representatives* (cf. Deut. 1:9; Num. 1:16; 11:16; 26:9). When Moses announced God's covenant, the binding and abiding relation between God and Israel, the people responded both directly and also through their elders that they would hear and obey (Exod. 3:16ff; 19:7ff).

When Israel called for a king to rule them a similar interplay took place. Even though Israel desired a king for the wrong motives, the Lord told Samuel to go along with what the people had chosen anyway (1 Sam. 8–10). Samuel then laid out the rights and duties of the king and Saul, whom God had already appointed, was chosen from among the people by lot.

The picture we get from these actions is not the modern one of popular sovereignty – whereby the people by virtue of their own inherent power choose and give authority to a ruler. It is clear throughout the Scriptures that political authority stems not from the people but from God. But political authority in Israel was also clearly not a dictatorship. The people shared in the responsibility of political office by choosing elders and then, through these elders, they chose kings and promised to obey and honour them. This is clear in the story of David. The elders came to David and told him that the Lord had appointed him to be the prince over Israel. They then entered into a covenant with David and annointed him as the king (2 Sam. 5:3).

The notion of covenant is a central one in the Bible and it is crucial to any understanding of political responsibility and office. Each party to a covenant agrees to certain conditions of a relationship between the parties and promises to uphold them. So the Lord promises to bless and multiply Israel, and Israel in turn promises to love the Lord and keep the commandments. This covenant must not be confused with the modern notion of contract – which is a legal relation established for the benefit of both parties. The covenant was not a deal, a *quid pro quo*. God even had covenant with the birds and cattle (Gen. 9:8–17). A covenant is a relation of mutual promise, commitment and responsibility, a relation that sets the pattern for life. Such covenants took place between God and Israel's kings and leaders (Ps. 132; 1 Kings 9:4, 5). As part of these commitments there were also covenants between the kings, the elders and the people (2 Sam. 5:3; Deut. 27).

In these covenants, which are all really only partial expressions of the one overriding Covenant, Israel as a people, as a body, takes it upon itself to uphold the law of the Lord. As part of this agreement the people of Israel, as a community, *all* agreed to take responsibility for what we would call their political affairs. All the people of Israel were responsible to see that justice was done. This was a responsibility they could not leave exclusively to their leaders. (Compare also Romans 13 and 1 Tim. 2:2).

Within this general scheme of commitment there were a variety of offices – specific roles with specific duties and authority. Those who filled these offices of priests, elders, judges or kings had duties, and the authority to carry out those duties, which were distinct from those of the people at large. But they were answerable to God and *to their fellows* in the context of the mutual responsibility of the covenant. The leaders and the people had a covenant together with God and *each other* to love God and to do justice by upholding God's just laws.

As revealed in the governing of Israel, and in the teaching on leadership and servanthood in the New Testament, the political task is one *given to the people as a whole*. Leaders and people are responsible to one another, and together we are responsible to God. This has major implications for how we should view the relation between government and the population at large in our own day.

It is true that the community of Israel was an intimately inter-woven pattern of religious, political, economic and social relations. We, on the other hand, live in a society where these aspects of life are much more diverse. This is perhaps to be expected in view of the increasing diversity of offices which grew throughout Israel's own history. In the modern world a variety of tasks are carried out through distinct institutions, such as the church or the state. It is also true that Israel was, despite its frequent turning away from God, much more homogeneous in terms of its culture and understanding of life than are the societies of modern states. But, despite these great differences between then and now, we may still say that the political order is designed by God to be a body of citizens, with diverse offices and responsibilities, called to implement justice within their territory.

This pattern of responsibility seems to be a continuing and abiding feature of the political order. It has manifested itself in a variety of different ways in political structures throughout history. But, even in those situations where kings or emperors or dictators have ruled with little restraint or concern for the welfare of the populace, such leaders still nearly always attempted to show that what they were doing was for the common good; that the leader somehow spoke *for* the population; that the leader, in some sense, *represented* the whole political order. This representation has been variously described as a divine or a historical mandate to govern, or else that the ruler was typical of the people (or else an outstanding example) and therefore spoke for those who were ruled. It has been the case that few rulers have cared to rule without at least *claiming* that they had some *popularly accepted reason for doing so*. The political order of God's world lends itself to some form of representative government.

So we can see that political authority is not portrayed in Scripture as 'a theocracy', as something apart from and laid on the population. Political authority is called to be an act of self government – an acceptance of God's law and a challenge to implement that law's just demands in the changing circumstances of life.

The Rule of Law

It should not bother us too much that the patterns in Scripture do not conform to modern ideas about the nature of democracy and the 'power of the people'. We have said that, in the Bible, power and authority do not stem from the people but from God. This sounds scandalous to modern ears and is usually described as some 'medieval' or 'theocratic' hangover. But it is neither. The fact that political authority stems not from the people but from God shows that the government does not have the right to do what it wills, and neither do the people. People are not just to express their own will in politics but are under the God-given mandate to do justice. One thing this means is that if a majority of the population wants to throw Jews and Gypsies into gas chambers, or to persecute minorities or otherwise to treat people unjustly, then these would *still not* be right things for governments to do. The will of the people, or of a majority of the people, does not make it right.

Of course no government should, or even can for long, go on its own merry way in complete defiance of the views of the population. The ability of governments to act justly and to carry out measures without resorting to totalitarianism depends on their being sensitive and responsive to the culture, opinion and wishes of the population. Yet it is still the government's task to act justly and not merely to be a bellweather of public opinion.

This view of justice is an important element of constitutional democracies. A constitution, written or unwritten, is a set of basic laws according to which a country is governed and to which all other laws are subordinate. Such a constitution is an attempt to recognise some fundamental order of justice to which the government must conform. It binds public opinion so that, at times, even if a majority of the population wants to do something then, if that something is not constitutional, it cannot be followed. Usually constitutional changes can be made only by a large and permanent shift in public opinion and with great deliberation. It is significant that in most countries with written constitutions the allegiance of the armed forces is, by law, not to the government or to popular will, but to the constitutional order itself. This is a recognition of the fact that there is an order to which *government and people* should conform.

In fact it is quite rare for any country to try to declare itself a 'pure democracy' in the sense that the only guide for government action is thought to be the will of the population. As soon as the population wills two contradictory things (such as many more government services combined with much lower taxes) which the government is, as a matter of democratic principle, forced to follow, then the structure immediately breaks down. Such 'pure democracy', as expressed, perhaps, in Rousseau's general will, easily deteriorates into the persecution of a minority by a majority. This persecution is often through a despotic leader who still maintains great popular support – Hitler and Mussolini were prime examples of this.

The Priority of Justice

At times even constitutional limits are not sufficient and great injustice can still be done even while following constitutional rules. This was the case with Hitler, who was able continually to get the support of huge majorities of Germans. These majorities were large enough to effect changes in the German constitution so that the Nazis could gradually and legally remake the German political structure in their own image. The Fuhrer legally could assume almost absolute power and then legally could disenfranchise and slaughter millions of people.

When trials of the Nazi leaders took place at Nuremberg, or even later as with Adolf Eichmann in Jerusalem, there was no actual basis in positive law – that is, law actually passed by governments – for trying them. They had technically broken no human law, constitutional or otherwise. In fact, if one held to the strict idea that laws are just humanly made things and that justice is only agreement among citizens, then there was no basis at all for trying them.

But it was clear that the Nazis *were* in violation of something fundamental and that their rank brutality cried out for a just retribution. In order to recognise this, the Nuremberg tribunal tried them on the basis of 'crimes against humanity'. This was a rather nebulous category and seems to have been coined in order to express the idea that there are fundamental and given rules for human conduct, while still trying to hang on to the modern humanist notion that humankind is free to make up its own rules as it goes along. (This was especially an act of hypocrisy on the part of the Russian judges at the tribunal, who represented a state which claimed that there could be no order for human conduct beyond a naked struggle for power between classes. In addition, Stalin had a rather impressive list of 'crimes against humanity' of his own). The events at Nuremberg still reveal that an idea of justice which transcends the will of majorities, or even the constitutional laws of states, is vital to the preservation of real human freedoms. In the extremes of political life we see that there must be an order beyond that of popular will.

Conclusion

The idea that political authority stems from God and not from 'the people' should not embarrass us. Nor should it cause us to seek to erect our own theocratic tyrannies. It is simply the recognition that people are not a law unto themselves but are called to do justice. We might add that constitutionalism is a good means of expressing this basic order of law while still maintaining the responsibility of government to the people. It would be too much to say that the Bible teaches constitutionalism, but I think it is fair to say that what the Bible reveals about the task of government can be well expressed in the modern age by means of a constitutional order (cf. 1 Sam. 10:25).

The co-responsibility of all people for the doing of justice obviously means that Christians are also co-responsible. We must take note of this very carefully. We Christians *are in fact responsible* for political doings. This means that we cannot be apolitical or politically uninvolved. We are *already* involved merely by virtue of living in God's world. If we try to be passive or to ignore what is happening about us then we are merely saying that we accept the way things are as being the way God wants them to be. If we try to be passive we are, in fact, expressing political views for we are accepting the situation *as it is*. Given the sin and suffering in the world such a political stance can only be viewed as sub-Christian, a turning away from what God and our neighbour ask of us. To be Christian we must take up our political responsibility and act in a way that moves governments to do justice.

SUMMARY

God has ordained an order to maintain just relations among people and between them and all other things in God's world. This order gradually evolves until it is represented by particular political office bearers who have authority from God through Jesus Christ to make laws to establish such justice. In a sinful world, these political authorities can, unlike individual people or other social institutions, compel people, by force if necessary, to obey such laws. The institutions which embody this political order continue to change and adapt through history, both because of human sin and also because of the necessity of dealing with new situations that require a just retribution.

The political order is neither the centre nor the most important institution in human affairs. It must be kept in its proper place and respect the authority of others to carry out their own particular responsibilities. Maintaining a just political order is the task of all the people within it: it is a communal authority and responsibility. While some people will have particular offices and will have more responsibility than others, these people are always responsible to the population at large for what they do.

While this order may take a particular form because of the presence of sin in the world, nevertheless it represents part of God's structuring of creation and mandating of human responsibility. As such, it represents a calling renewed by the gospel and which will be completely healed and restored to its full task at the coming of the Lord.

This is, very generally, what we learned of politics in reading the Scriptures. In terms of this picture, we must understand the purpose of our political involvement. Christianly inspired politics is not intended to defend or to convert people to the Christian faith, although we can hope that it might help in that. Christian political action is not intended to show the faults of non-Christians in politics or to show the superiority of Christianity in politics, although it might even help in that also. Christian political action is to be neither of these. It flows simply from the recognition that we, along with all the rest of humankind, are responsible for the stewardship of and the development of life in the creation. Our politics is one part of our multifaceted task within the creation: it is taking up our responsibility to establish just relations between all the other responsibilities in the world, defending the poor, the needy and the oppressed, rewarding both good and evil.

As we try to carry out this task we must have some ongoing sense of what just relations are. We must know what the relations between things in God's world in the latter part of the twentieth century ought to be. This in turn implies that we must have a Christian view not only of politics but also of the world itself in order to have some means of working out our faith in actual, present political realities. It is to this 'working out' of the Christian faith in modern society that we will now turn our attention.

4: Understanding the Modern World

CHRISTIAN DIRECTION

The Focus of Christian Action

Christians are often quick to point out that 'we don't have a hot line to God' in politics. By this is meant that we can't baptise our current political opinions and endeavours as the only possible Christian understanding. When this sentiment is expressed in this way it is impossible to disagree with it. We certainly need humility about all our human efforts, politics included. But while we must recognise that Christians disagree on politics, as they do on a host of other things, we should not accept such disagreement as a fact of life about which we can and should do nothing. While it is true that we are not united on political matters, and perhaps that we never shall be, yet this is a situation that we must strive to *overcome*, not accept, just as we must strive to overcome differences about the authority of the Bible or on the nature of salvation. Merely to *accept* such disagreement would be a failure to take either the Lordship of Christ or the authority of the Word of God seriously. Such passive acceptance would be a confession that either the Bible does not speak about politics, or that the Bible is not clear about what it says, or that we are unwilling to hear what it says. I will leave the last of these options to the heart of the reader and make some comments about the first two.

As I tried to show in the last chapter, political responsibility and justice are intimately intertwined and there are several hundred references in the Scriptures to justice in all its manifestations. Hence, it is clear that we cannot say that the Bible does not address politics. The Bible spends more time talking about political doings than it does about charismatic gifts, or the return of Christ. My point is not that these other things are unimportant, for they are vitally important. Rather, my point is that the Scriptures speak to us continually, incessantly and unremittingly about justice and politics. We cannot take the view that the Bible is silent on these matters.

We are then left with the question as to whether the Bible is clear about what it says. Of course, clarity has as much to do with the reader as it does with the text, and there are many different traditions of Bible reading. But no Christian should accept the easy relativism, or even 'situational ethics', that in fact will ultimately prevail if we are content merely to say 'some people say this and some people say that' or 'there is truth on both sides'. If the Bible seems unclear, and it often does, then we must continually, persistently and unrelentingly struggle to understand and follow its message (for at heart the Bible is *one* message). We must continually question and test out views. While divisions will always be hard to overcome, and will not finally be overcome until Christ returns, we can no more passively accept those divisions than we can passively accept divisions about the nature of salvation and faith. Political sanctification, like all sanctification, is a process that is usually long, painful and unfinished: but it is a process to which we are persistently called.

Certainly we cannot act as though the Bible leaves us with only the bare command to love one another and that then we must take it from there. The Scriptures are full of the revelation of what love actually *means* in the various dimensions and situations of human life. Love requires us to be *just* in our dealings with our fellows. Love requires us to be *stewardly* in our use of our time and possessions. Love requires us to be *faithful* in our covenant with God and faithful in our dealings with others. Love requires us to be *truthful* and speak fairly and honestly of our neighbours and ourselves.

In turn, the meaning of justice, of stewardship, of faithfulness, of truthfulness is further amplified in the Scriptures. Justice requires equity, fair measure, a chance for a hearing and the defence of the poor and oppressed. Laid out before us throughout the Scriptures for our example are the words that God spoke to the chosen people telling them how to live properly and lovingly as keepers of the earth and unfolders of history. We are not adrift on a sea of mere opinions wherein we can say nothing specific from the gospel about politics. The *law* revealed in Scripture is *itself* an exposition of what love means (cf. 1 John 3:19–24; 5:1–5).[2]

Thus, we do not participate politically on the basis of 'neutral reason' or 'common sense'. God has given us direction, has revealed to us what politics is about and has told us what justice means. We should not enter politics as idealistic moralists who simply want to do good. If this was all we were we would soon be cast about by the winds of public opinion. We should not merely reflect the opinions of those we work with, or the interests of our class. No, we are to act politically as witnesses to a gospel, as political followers of Jesus Christ, as ones who have tried to learn at least something of what God calls human society and the political order to be.

Nor is a knowledge of God's law enough. We do not shed our Christian *faith* when we enter the political arena. We are to enter as witnesses to a Saviour who is also the Saviour of politics. Our politics must live out and flow from and witness to our faith. Any lasting healing in politics will not come from merely borrowing Christian 'principles', be they human equality, care for the poor, or individual responsibility, as if they existed as moral imperatives independent of the gospel. It will only come through actual living faith in Jesus Christ, who is the One who gives life to the law, including the law as it is expressed in politics. Whatever party affiliation we may, or may not, have, we should not enter politics as ones content to be liberals, socialists, or conservatives, or Tories, Labourites or Alliance members. Rather, we must enter as ones who seek to bear witness to and to serve the healing power of Jesus Christ in the political ministry that God has provided.

The freedom of Christian action

Our Christian political action is to be not only focussed but also free. One reason that Christians are divided about politics is the fact that politics, unlike physics or geology, deals with relations that people themselves have shaped. Political institutions reflect God's ordering of creation but they also reflect human choices and therefore they *change* over time. But our usual ways of reading the Bible have often left us poorly equipped to deal with *changing* realities and *free* choices. On the one hand, we tend to say that everything must be done in the same way as it was in the Bible, which, in our very different world, appears to be a hopeless dream. Or, on the other hand, we tend to say that, because the situation is very different now, then the Bible doesn't really speak to it, which is a hopeless abdication.

Both of these views are wrong because an essential part of the teaching of Scripture is precisely the importance of change, of history, of human responsibility, of human freedom. An essential part of being bound to the Word of God is being free to work out the service of God. As we have seen, there is a development of human life and society as portrayed throughout the Scriptures. Part of this development has to do with changes in political structure and authority. We go from Cain to Abraham to Moses. As we read through the history of Israel we learn more fully what God is about and we see new political forms, such as judges, kings and prophets, appearing as new circumstances develop. Through Abraham, through Moses, through Jesus, we gradually learn more of what the implications of justice are.

There is no reason to expect this process to stop at the end of biblical revelation. Indeed, the teaching of the 'cultural mandate' shows us that *history*, change and development is very real and very much part of God's intention for human life. We are charged to create, develop and adapt what is about us in response to the guidance that God has given us. God's revelation of the nature of politics as an act of ministry is not given so that we should slavishly imitate the patterns of government found in, for example, the Old Testament. As members of the body of Christ, *we too* are mandated by God, we too must take up *our own responsibility* as shapers of the world. The whole point of being human, of being made in the image of God, is that we are given *responsibility* for the earth. We have to make real decisions about how we can put flesh on what God has shown us to be the path of peace, hope, stewardship and justice.

The mere fact that we are responsible creatures shows that our task is not a fixed and determined one with no room for freedom of implementation. In fact, the same responsibility and freedom of decision occurs throughout the biblical record. At times we read of people faithful to God who varied the requirements of the law in order better to fulfil its purpose. For example, King Hezekiah was a man 'who did what was right in the eyes of the Lord' (2 Chr. 29:2). Because of the many sins of the people and the impending wrath of God, Hezekiah needed to move very quickly in order to reestablish Israel's obedience to its covenant with God (29:5–10, 36). Because he was in such hurry he allowed the Levites to help the priests in sacrificing the animals presented to the Lord, something which had not been allowed in the law of Moses. Shortly afterwards Hezekiah interceded with the Lord to ask pardon for these acts. He said that they were the acts of those who had 'set their heart to seek God'. Then, again, contrary to the law of Moses, he allowed those who were not purified to eat of the sacrifices which had been made. At the end of all this 'the Lord heard Hezekiah and healed the people' (2 Chr. 30:17–20).

Perhaps the starkest example is that of Jesus when faced with the question of divorce. The Pharisees asked Jesus: 'Is it lawful to divorce one's wife for any cause?' Jesus answered that God had made man and woman to be one from the beginning of creation and so 'What therefore God has joined together let no man put asunder'. The Pharisees then asked, referring to Deuteronomy 24:4, 'Why then did Moses command one to give a certificate of divorce, and to put her away?' Jesus replied again 'For your hardness of heart Moses allowed you to divorce your wives, but from the beginning it was not so' (Matt. 19:3–9).

Admittedly it was Jesus himself who said this and one could argue that Jesus could do things in relation to the law that we cannot. But what Jesus did was to give an example of how properly to read the law. He says that God, from the creation itself, has put man and woman together and that they should not be separated. But, because sinful people could not manage this complete restriction, Moses allowed them to divorce in order to avoid even worse problems. In reading the law Jesus goes to God's basic intent ['from the beginning this was not so'] and he reads the law given through Moses as a way of expressing this intent in a particular circumstance ['Moses allowed you']. Moses had to take the sinful situation into account.

From this we can develop an understanding of how to read the law and we can learn to give expression to God's law in the particular circumstances we are in. Indeed, as Wenham points out, the Mosaic law also contains examples of its own application to particular situations.[1] The law is not just 'principles' which we apply to our 'particulars'. Most of the law is *itself* the working out of such principles in a variety of life situations. In the law the Ten Commandments (and, more so, the two great Commandments of love) are central and most of the rest of Deuteronomy is 'case law', law that comments on what is central and applies and works it out in particular situations. The law is developed in terms of concrete reality. This is not to say that God's commandment changes, but rather that the commandment must be expressed in such a way that its intent is fulfilled. The implementation of the law is always the implementation of God's abiding order of and for justice in the concrete and variable situations of our lives.

The modern implementation of justice as revealed in God's word will always be difficult, simply because of the complexity of unravelling the core of a commandment from its expression in a particular age. Nevertheless this difficulty is itself a continuing facet of our human responsibility.

Understanding God's World

Learning politically as Christians is not only a matter of a more complex understanding of or interpretion of the Scriptures. We must understand not only God's Word but *God's world*. We cannot, nor should we want to, find all the answers to all our questions in the Bible. While one can certainly repair a car in a

Christian way, and while the Bible certainly directs us so that we should know what car repair is all about (the use of technical gifts in service to our neighbour, petrol-conserving cars only), yet none of us would want a mechanic who knows nothing but Bible texts! A good mechanic, a *Christian* mechanic, must know of the potentialities and the structure of the engine. He or she must know what a car is and how it works.

The Scriptures are not some divinely inspired *Encyclopedia Britannica* wherein all human knowledge is found in Godly form. They are not given to tell us *everything* but they are focussed on a particular message – on telling us who God is, who we are, how we came into being, what we live for, how and why we do evil and know suffering, and especially how God has prepared and wrought our salvation. They are given for our edification and directing, to open our hearts to our Creator and Redeemer and to direct us in obedient and life-giving ways. God's word is a lamp unto our feet, a light on our path (Psalm 119:105). A lamp is not given so it can be stared at but so it can be used to *illuminate something else*. The Scriptures are to be shone ahead of us on the path on which we walk. The Scriptures are to guide us in discovering God's world, so that we can understand it aright. Thus, to act biblically is not necessarily to act in strict limitation of a specific biblical happening; it also means to act in historical continuity with that happening.

Indeed it was a neglect of this fact that has caused many of the problems of the Church in Britain today. The decline in the influence of Christian social teaching parallels the development of the industrial revolution. Christian social teaching declined in large part because it was not able to give guidance in a new and rapidly changing situation. The examples from the Old and New Testaments are in farming settings. They refer to rents, land boundaries, gleaning fields and so forth. Hence, their relevance to our own situation was more easily seen when this country was largely rural. However, unless one is able to take these same examples and discern their meaning in a world of capital, of factories, of division of labour, of unions and of mass production, then they will rapidly appear to be totally irrelevant. This irrelevance quickly became obvious to most economists at the time of the industrial revolution and they promptly declared their science to be free from moral concerns and advocated a science of economics in which a concern for justice was external, if not irrelevant.

Christian political service requires understanding the world in the light of the Scriptures. We must uncover new things, learn new facts, respond to new situations and devise new plans as we are directed by God's Word. The world is not something that just happens to be there: it is something that God made with human-kind in mind. As God has created the world good, then the very way this world is made speaks to us of its Creator. Even though twisted by and caked in sin, the creation has not lost its character as the expression of God's will. In fact, as Paul says, the creation itself is also God's revelation to us (Romans 1:18–21; 1 Tim. 4:1–5). We must learn from God's revelation to us both in the Scriptures and, in the light of those Scriptures, in the world. We proceed not only deductively from the teaching of the Scriptures but also *developmentally* and *obediently* in discovering what the Lord says to us in the works round about us.

Clearly as most of the things that exist in modern politics (elections, civil services, policies, parliaments, parties) did not occur in biblical times, we cannot determine a political policy solely by a process of biblical exegesis. We cannot prooftext a solution to the Falklands/Malvinas, we must know the situation itself. However, what we can do is try to approach such questions guided by biblical revelation. We can try to discover what God requires *now* of us, responsible stewards of the earth, in the modern age.

One thing this means is that Christian political understanding and action is never an exercise whose answers and strategies are known before we begin. Its end is not predetermined (except in the final sense of Christ's ultimate victory and the renewal of all things). Our politics always involves real questioning, probing, trying, learning and revising as we struggle to learn and to do God's will in the historical situation we are in.

What follow in this chapter are attempts to develop criteria for such questioning. They are attempts to outline how we should understand the political world about us, attempts at a beginning biblical analysis of the world, attempts at *continuing* our cultural mandate.

THE NEED FOR CHRISTIAN SOCIAL ANALYSIS

Facts and Values

A biblical understanding of the world directs us to know not only justice, stewardship, faithfulness, a concern for the poor and a love for our enemies, it also directs us to know the nature of governments, the structures of society, the function of law, and the patterns and meaning of history. Hence it is wrong to think that our Christian faith provides us only with 'values' that we then 'plug into' the 'facts' in order to get strategies.

The content of biblical faith is not just some moral norms to apply to our situation, it is a way of seeing and understanding that situation itself. For example, we should not take certain Christian 'values', such as love or justice, and then try to work them out in international relations via either a Marxist analysis of world trade or a systems theory of international interraction, or a neo-conservative or Keynesian theory of political economy, or a behaviouralist or functionalist theory of the state. Rather we must seek, as much as we can, to ensure that even the very categories with which we analyze and interpret our situation are shaped by our biblical faith. If we fail to do this then we will find that our attempted Christian approach to the world will be shaped more by the analysis we pick up than it will be by our faith itself. This can be illustrated by the example of Liberation Theology.

Liberation Theology

Liberation Theology is an interpretation of the Christian faith shaped by decades of suffering and oppression in Latin America.[2] Theologians and priests, many of them from Europe, found themselves among people in deep poverty and misery, in societies with vast disparities of wealth, and political regimes which existed to maintain this situation rather than to seek justice. You work with a family in a city where the husband was picked up by the police a month ago. You try to find out where he is, or even if he is alive. Then it happens again and again, until you realise that you face not only a pastoral problem but an organised repression which must be resisted.

You work with peasants seeking food until you realise that the food lands are all tied up in plantations and *latifundias* (landed estates) which produce non-food crops such as coffee and sugar for export to rich countries. You realise that the problem is not lack of food or land but the way in which it is owned and distributed.

Your training seems totally foreign to this situation. Theological discussions in the rich lands appear to be sterile academic affairs, far removed from your own calling in oppressed countries. Politics and economics dominate the situation, and when, and if, you enter politics in opposition to the oppression, the Marxists and socialists are the only ones already there, and what they say appears to fit the situation.

From out of this crucible, Liberation Theology was born. It is intended to be a theology oriented not to abstract theological theories but to concrete action, to commitment to the poor, to politics, to liberation from oppression, to justice as a central element of the gospel. It is prominent in the revolution in Nicaragua and in the present civil war in El Salvador.

Because of the situation in which it developed, I am reluctant to say anything, let alone anything critical, about Liberation Theology. It is, after all, one of its own principal tenets that this theology has *grown from experience* – and that one who does not share this experience cannot speak to it. Such theologians are, rightfully, impatient with discursive critiques of their work from more comfortable lands. And, as I have never experienced such a situation, I have no wish to pass judgment on those who have.

But it is also true that most liberation theologians are well qualified academically, are proficient in Hebrew and Greek, can write dense Marxist prose, and in general give evidence of owing a great debt to the more radically inclined European intellectuals, especially Marxists. It would be a mistake to see Liberation Theology as only emerging full blown from Latin American experience for such theology has clear, well established roots in the traditions of Western radicalism. Coupled with this is the fact that Liberation Theology has now become widespread in the industrialised west, especially among liberal theologians but also among evangelicals. As I live in and experience *this* world, including its underside, I feel I can make some judgements about such theology when it is present in the western, industrialised world, and this I will do.

In their great desire to escape theological sterility, liberation theologians have preached that abstract talk of justice will not do and, hence, that theology must be supplemented by social, political and economic analysis in order to apply it to the concrete world. They speak of Christian 'values' which need social analysis in order to get at the 'facts'. But just any social analysis won't do for Christian action, because the so-called 'value-free' social sciences, dominant especially in Western Europe and North America, are rejected as the tools and self-images of an increasingly controlling and manipulative capitalist society. A different social analysis is sought, one which will highlight the system of oppression. The analysis that is chosen is usually Marxist.

There are diverging views as to why Marxist analysis is selected. Some suggest that such tools of analysis are really a 'science', value-free and objective, hence they can be used by Christians as instruments whose use is independent of any faith. Another view admits that Marxist analysis is committed and 'value-laden', as is all of science, but maintains that, since Marxism has an ethos or outlook similar to that of Christianity, that is, a search for justice, its analysis is one that is admirably suitable for Christian concerns.

But, for either set of reasons, we end up with Christian 'values' supplemented by Marxist 'analysis'.

The Liberation Theology argument runs like this: theology is only good if it stands with the poor and expresses their interests. But, to know what these interests really are one must have a social analysis. The suitable social analysis is Marxist. However, in such a scheme, it is the *analysis* which *determines* the perceived *situation* of the poor, out of which one then acts. All the emphasis on theology arising out of experience and on learning from the poor should not obscure this fact. If the poor feel their real interest happens to be in supporting a military junta to preserve stability, or in getting 2% more money next year, or in being left alone to hope for heaven, then this view will likely not be adopted by liberation theologians who believe that only Marxism shows the roots of poverty – exploitation – and shows the only way – class struggle. The result is that members of the poor need to be brought round to Marxist views. This process may be called education, consciousness raising, conscientisation, or what you will, but liberation theologians usually have at least some strategy shaped by their analysis beyond which they will not go.

The resulting strategy is then shaped like this: tools of analysis determine the perceived situation of the poor, which then determines the theology of liberation. But, in such a scheme, the 'theology' can have no real critical input into the analysis that ultimately determines its content. The content of Christian faith is then only a 'commitment', a 'value', that provides the *dynamic* but not the *content* of the process. The content of the strategy is determined by the analysis chosen. Indeed Hugo Assman describes theology as the 'second word' which follows the 'first word' of the social sciences. And, since 'tools of analysis' do not fall fully formed from the sky, but are an expression of a whole view of the nature of humankind, of the world, of history, of justice, of wealth, of work, of destiny, of salvation, then the Marxist tail will wag the Christian dog. Christian faith does not add anything distinctive to the scheme, it only tells us to do 'good' while other forces will tell us what actually is the 'good' to be sought.

Other Approaches

I have taken the example of Liberation Theology not because I want to condemn it but because it most clearly illustrates the crucial nature of the relation between faith and social analysis. The tendency of Christians to borrow from and in turn to be shaped by analyses with roots far from the Christian faith is endemic to far more than Liberation Theology. A few further examples will suffice.

While the great French, Christian sociologist, Jacques Ellul, has certainly contributed his own distinct elements to sociology, yet the influence of Marx on his thought is quite amazing. He was a professing Marxist for only a short period of time in his youth, but Marx's influence still remains with him. Ellul himself refers to his 'twofold intellectual origin in Marx and Barth',[3] particularly with respect to his own view of dialectics as the basic structuring principle of society, history and, indeed, the creation itself. In turn Barth and Ellul have become two of the dominant influences on the most persuasive current anabaptist theologian, John Howard Yoder. These three have then become some of the major influences (excluding the many biblical and more ancient ones!) on much of the anabaptist revival associated with magazines such as *Sojourners* and with the current stresses on Christian non-violent action and anti-militarism.

On the other hand, Sir Fred Catherwood leans heavily on the German sociologist Max Weber. He borrows Weber's theory on the relation between protestantism and capitalism as a basic means of interpreting the causes of economic progress in various countries.[4] Alternatively, Jerry Falwell, the leader of the 'Moral Majority' in the United States, like so many conservative Christians, including those on this side of the Atlantic, borrows most of his views of the economic duties of governments from free-enterprise economists. His favourite is the recent Nobel Prize winner, Milton Friedman, of the University of Chicago. Indeed, for one who claims to be a fundamentalist, Falwell seems markedly reluctant to make any consistent reference to the Bible on these matters.[5]

These few brief examples could easily be multiplied. My basic point is that, in borrowing such forms of analysis, Christians already determine much of the content of the proposals they will offer as policies stemming from the gospel. I am not suggesting that any and all of these analyses are totally wrong, but I am saying that we must have clear grounds for adopting any particular means of interpreting what is happening in our world and, further, that we must develop means of understanding society which themselves flow from our Christian faith.

At this point in the book I should perhaps go on to describe such means of Christian social analysis. But I shall not do so, for the simple and embarrassing reason that such means do not exist, at least not in any well developed way.[6] However, in the next section of this chapter I will try to give a broad overview of some insights for understanding societies, and then in the chapters on political economy and international relations, I shall develop further themes specific to those fields.

Developing such analysis remains a task crucial to any enduring Christian politics. No doubt readers will be able to discern foreign and unbiblical elements and assumptions in what I write here (as elsewhere). But, only as we continue to (gently) expose and critique these elements in one another can we move beyond them and hope to develop an integrally Christian understanding of the world we live in.

IDOLATRY AND CREATION

Life Is Religion

We saw earlier how *all* action in God's world can be and should be a service to God and our neighbours. There is therefore no specific *area* of life which we can call 'religious' as though other areas of life were not 'religious'. To put it briefly, we may say that 'life is religion', that our religion is what we believe, think, say and do each and every moment of our lives.[7] As one friend remarked 'I can tell more about your faith from reading your cheque-book than your prayer-book'. Everything we do is religion in that it is done in faithfulness or in unfaithfulness to God.

This is true not only for Christians, but also for Jews or Hindus, and also for each and every other person. We *all, all of human-kind*, are made in the image of God. That image, though stained and twisted by sin, still distinguishes each human person. All people participate in the cultural mandate, either in obedience or disobedience to God. If this were not so then no human life would be possible, for human life is itself the imaging of God within the creation.

This means that we should never consider a person, a corporation, a book, or a government as 'non-religious'. They are always religious in that they reflect either a turning toward God or a turning away from God in their activities. Of course they may not know that and they may even deny it, they usually do in fact, but it still remains true. Everybody serves somebody. If people do not serve God, then they will serve something else. The 'some-things else' that people serve are what the Bible calls 'idols'.[8]

Idols

The history of Israel is full of references to 'idols', 'graven images' and 'high places'. Israel's sin is always that it turns away from

God and turns to idols. We might even say that idolatry is not just another sin alongside the rest but is a particular way of speaking about all sin. All sin is an expression of the basic sin of idolatry, of putting something else in the place of God. This is one reason why idolatry is the theme which opens the ten commandments – 'You shall have no other gods besides me. You shall not make for yourselves a graven image . . .' (Exod. 20:3, 4).

In the Scriptures no one is an atheist: rather, if someone does not worship and serve God, then they will inevitably worship and serve another 'god'. These other 'gods' are things within the creation, either already there or else made by human hands. They are things that we worship and serve, things that we trust in, things that we rely on to save us. Habbakuk says:

What profit is an idol when its maker has shaped it, a metal image, a teacher of lies? For the workman trusts in his own creation when he makes dumb idols (2:18).

Paul describes idols as 'a representation by the art and the imagination of man' (Acts 17:29) and he condemns 'worshipping the creature rather than the creator' (Romans 1:24). Idolatry is putting a created thing in the place of the Creator.

An idol is a thing which humans create or find and which they then *trust in*. The worshipping of idols is never a purely formal matter, like having a little shrine in the living room. Such worship is, like all worship (Romans 12:1; James 1:27), an act of one's life. Idolatry is serving something other than God, *it is putting our final trust in anything within the creation*. Whatever apart from God that we hold to be the core or key to our problems is an idol.

Idolatry is manifested in many ways. When the prophets speak of it they put it together in a list of acts of pride and oppression. Isaiah says,

For thou hast rejected thy people,
the house of Jacob,
because they are full of diviners
from the east
and soothsayers like the Philistines,
and they strike hands with foreigners.
Their land is filled with silver
and gold,
and there is no end to their treasures;
their land is filled with horses,

and there is no end to their chariots,
Their land is filled with idols;
they bow down to the works
of their hands
to what their fingers have made (2:6–8).

The list of sins which Isaiah gives is a list of different ways of describing the basic sin of turning away from God. The house of Jacob gives heed to false gods (through diviners and soothsayers), it picks up ways other than the ways God has taught them (compromising with foreigners), it seeks wealth and security (gold and silver) rather than God, it relies on military might rather than God (chariots – the means of attack, the means of *aggressive*, not defensive warfare). All of this is summed up in Isaiah's final saying that the land is filled with idols. The list is a variety of ways of saying the same thing. Just as Habakkuk condemns the workman 'trusting in his own creation', so Isaiah condemns 'trust in chariots' (31:1). A chariot, military power, can be an idol as potent as, or as useless as, Baal, Moloch or Ashtaroth. The worship of money, the act of relying on money for peace or health, is quite simply mammon-worship. And Jesus says 'No man can worship two masters' (Matt. 6:24).

We should look at the supposedly secular and rational world about us with this understanding of idols in mind. Then we would echo Paul's cry to the philosophical idolators at Athens: 'I perceive that in every way you are very religious' (Acts 17:22). All around us are people and governments *believing*, *trusting* deep down in their hearts, putting their lives on the line for the hope that more military power will bring peace, or that more wealth will bring happiness, or that more education will bring tolerance, or that the laws of history will bring a new society. All of these beliefs are what the Bible calls idolatry.

It is not that legitimate defence, or money, or learning, or change are wrong. All things in the creation are given for our good and are to be used rightly. But none of these can be a cause of hope, or a foundation of peace, or a source of love. None of them can be trusted in or relied upon to save us. All of them find their proper place only when approached humbly in reliance upon *God's* faithfulness, justice and mercy.

Idols, ancient and modern, always have an effect upon those that worship them. The Psalmist describes this effect:

The idols of the nations are silver and gold,
the work of men's hands.

They have mouths but they speak
not,
they have ears but they hear not,
they have eyes but they see not,
nor is there any breath in their mouths.
Those that trust in them are like them!
Yea, everyone who trusts in them.
(Ps. 135:15–18. Emphasis added.)

As the Psalmist says, we become like our idols. We create them, but then we, in turn, become transformed into *their* image. And, as we are the moulders of history and the shapers of society, then we will shape our society into the pattern of the idols, the 'gods' that we worship. In what we build and create we give expression to the intentions and hopes of our hearts.

From out of his consideration of idolatry the Christian economist, Bob Goudzwaard, formulated three basic rules to try to explain the connection between our worship of God or 'gods' and our theoretical and practical pursuits.[9] The rules are:

(1) Everyone serves god(s) with their lives
(2) Everyone is transformed into an image of their god
(3) Mankind creates and forms a structure of society in its own image and, hence, into the image of its idols.

Idolatry and Creation

With these three basic rules we have the beginning germ of a Christian interpretation of society and societies. While obviously not specific enough for most of the tasks at hand, they do provide an orientation, a way of opening up the dynamics of social structures and ways of life. We should combine these rules with our knowledge that God orders the creation – that the world, including social life, is made in a certain way and produces blessing when God's laws for life are followed. This combination gives us the following picture of the world.

God has made the world good. All things in creation can be and should be used to love God and our fellows. God has told us to shape and build the world and has given us diverse tasks such as being parents, administering justice, growing crops and praying. But because of sin, we turn from our Creator and try to put something else, be that power, security, sex, status, science, solidarity or whatever, in the place of God. We begin to shape our world around this false 'god', we put other things in creation into the service of that 'god' and we produce corruption, distortion and oppression.

Any Christian social analysis must then seek to understand at least two things:

1. The good things that God has put in the world, which endure and can give healing despite human sin;
2. The turning of these good things into idols which people worship and which twist and distort that creation, causing destruction and pain.

These should be part of our basic framework for understanding the role of law, the nature of economics, the function of democracy, the goals of foreign policy, or anything else in modern politics.

UNDERSTANDING POLITICAL PARTIES AND MOVEMENTS

This beginning framework of creation and idolatry can help us understand political parties and how we should relate to them. Political parties always have a two-fold character. One part, related to their religious commitment, is a vision of human life and salvation. The other part, related to the fact that they, like all of us, live in God's creation, is a recognition of real problems and a programme to combat those problems.

On the side of religious commitment, we find that political parties are never just groupings of people who claim to have some good ideas about what may be best for the country, they always express a basic view of what is important in life, what the root of evil is and what the purpose of politics is. That this is true of our current parties in the matter of economics will be shown in our next chapter. For the moment we will just say that parties ultimately always reveal a vision of life, either in the service of God or of an idol.

This is most clearly shown by revolutionary parties. Such parties are never just oriented to combatting injustice, though certainly this may be part of their goal, but they always maintain that they possess some 'key' which will create a 'new man' and hence a 'new society' in which the problems of the past will be definitively overcome. They rely on some 'God', whether that be Evolution, Nature, Progress, Society, Reason, History, the Individual, or whatever.[10] The French Revolution was thoroughly religious in character, as was perhaps most clearly revealed when a prostitute was dressed up as the goddess REASON, put in place on the altar in the Cathedral of Notre Dame in Paris, and worshipped by the surrounding crowd.

The same impulses come to the fore in the American, Russian and Chinese revolutions and in the development of Fascism and Nazism. They are present in the Sandinistas in Nicaragua and the Khmer Rouge of Cambodia. Such movements never ultimately define themselves only in terms of concrete political goals such as land reform, regular elections, or literacy programmes, but in terms of an overarching vision of a new society. If we try to understand revolutionary movements only as responses to injustice then we will fail to understand them.

What is true of revolutionary movements is also true of conservative and middle-of-the-road parties. The only difference (apart from the content of the programme itself!) is that revolutionaries, and strong Conservatives such as Mrs Thatcher, have the courage of their convictions whereas those in the middle tend to waffle and try to cover up their tracks. Nevertheless, an examination of their programmes and speeches always reveals some vision of what human salvation is about. The recent speech by Neil Kinnock, the leader of the Labour party, is a good example: 'When we organise . . . we do it for socialism because we know that only socialism holds as the jewel of its whole purpose the liberation, the emancipation of humankind.'[11] There is scarcely a political manifesto available, and hardly a major political speech given, that does not call explicitly for 'faith' in some principle or programme and which does not claim to be the foundation for a 'new order' of things. Human beings are inescapably religious and this always shows in their politics.

But, at the same time, politics, like all human activity, is never defined completely by the religious commitments of its members. For all human activity takes place in God's creation and is always shaped and limited by the nature of that creation. People may try to pretend that they are gods, but they will never be able to act as gods because they remain fixed as human beings in God's world. In the same way, human political activity can never completely lose its God-given nature as a search for a just ordering of society. Political programmes must always deal with the creation that we all share. The French and Russian revolutions were an outcry at the suffering of the poor and a revolt against the oppression they suffered. The Sandinistas rightfully overthrew the tyrant, Somoza, and have begun literacy and redistribution programmes. Current politics are also genuine attempts to formulate practical solutions to real problems.

Hence, when we consider political parties and programmes, we must consider this two-fold character of a religious commitment combined with a genuine search for justice. Our own attitudes toward existing political parties will also reflect this dual character. We may support many things in a party's programme but, unless such a party is committed to giving political expression to the gospel of Jesus Christ, we can never ultimately feel comfortable with its view of what will solve human problems. For example, it is quite possible that we would feel, along with the Labour Party, that the government needs to be more active in combatting unemployment or in redistributing income, or that we need unilateral nuclear disarmament. But no Christian should believe that a stress on human equality or on the primacy of 'society' over the 'individual' is itself any key to human happiness. Similarly, we might believe with the Tories that government control is too all-pervasive and, hence, needs to be restricted. But no Christian should believe that reliance on human freedom and individual initiative is any key to human happiness. Hence our attitudes towards existing political parties may be critically supportive but they must always retain a deeper level of detachment. If we are serious about our faith, then we must have the courage to insist that it alone can be the bringer of justice.

By itself, of course, our discussion of idolatry does not provide all of our political questions, let alone provide many of the answers, but it can provide some help in illuminating our world. In chapter V, on economics, and chapter VI, on international relations, I will attempt to show in some more detail how this can be done.

DEALING WITH 'MORAL' QUESTIONS

The Issues Selected

In this book I discuss only *two* political issues – the welfare state and the nuclear arms race – at any length. However, I would also like to suggest possibilities for dealing with some other matters. Consequently, I will make some remarks about how we should approach what are called 'moral' questions, such as abortion, pornography and censorship. I will not try to provide 'answers' to these matters, but only ways of approaching them. To do this we will need to review the meaning of 'justice', the meaning of 'human rights', and the task of government.

Justice and Rights

We said earlier (chapter 3E) that it is not the task of governments to set everything right but that people in a variety of life situations have their own responsibilities and authority, an authority which governments must respect. The mere fact that someone is doing something bad is not itself grounds for government action. The fact that persons, families, churches, unions and business enterprises have their own authority and responsibility means that they must have the freedom to exercise that responsibility. All of us act in ways that are sinful and if it were the task of government to always correct and forbid us then we would soon end up in a totalitarian system where none of us were free to make any real decisions at all nor to exercise any real responsibility for good or ill. This biblical theme is one that is pointed to by the modern idea of *human rights* – that human beings must be free of political control in many areas of their life, regardless of whether we like what they are doing or not. So, for example, the mere fact that pornography or abortion may be evil is not itself grounds for government action. In this sense we should agree that it is not the task of government to enforce morality, even, or especially, Christian morality. The government's task is to enforce that particular part of morality that we call justice. Governments must respect human callings, human responsibilities, human rights.

But, as well as asserting the importance of human *freedom* even if it results in bad things, we must also assert the importance of *justice* as the way in which human freedoms must be related to one another. Relations between people, institutions, organisations and things are also and always subject to justice. We cannot believe in any absolute rights apart from how they affect others. We must always ensure that relations *between* things in society are just. What people write or see or do cannot be treated as completely their own affair for their real freedoms must always be exercised in the context of just relations with others. Consequently, while we must place high value on free expression and on the right of people to control their own bodies, we cannot accept the idea that, for example, censorship is always wrong or that abortion should not be legislated against. These activities, like all human activities, must be tested in terms of whether they maintain justice.

Pornography

Let us consider the instance of pornography. It is produced largely for men and portrays women. The major theme of such pornography, as is becoming apparent in the latest spate of videos, is not sexuality but violence and, in particular, sexual violence. We are witnessing a vast outpouring of books, magazines and films that revel in the rape, humiliation, torture and death of women.

In this situation the freedom of people to produce and consume what they want is not the only concern. We must also consider the rights of women, who, as the crime statistics show, are themselves being *actually* subjected to increased pain, humiliation and rape. Justice requires the state to protect women from any social effects from pornography.

Of course there are ongoing debates between social scientists about the effects of pornography and some maintain that it provides a harmless outlet for aggression which might otherwise be acted out. But many of the earlier studies, such as the Danish ones, tended to be produced by people who were ideologically committed to opposing censorship, and are now being discredited. It now seems clearer that pornography does in fact promote the acceptance of violence against women.

Consider the analogy of violence against blacks or Pakistanis. What would our reaction be if there were a multi-billion pound industry portraying blacks or 'Pakis' being beaten, tortured and killed, while at the same time increasing numbers of them were being attacked. The matter would clearly be one of defending the civil rights of such minorities. Women require equal protection for their rights also.

Even if one could not show a link between pornographic violence and actual assaults on women we would still have to consider legislation about pornography because of people's feelings. Growing up and living in a culture that swarms with portrayals of you being degraded is itself a humiliating and degrading situation, a situation that calls for redress, including government redress.

Consequently we must deal with matters such as censorship and pornography not by asserting that governments should stamp out whatever is evil nor by asserting some absolute rights of free expression. Rather we must both protect human freedom and establish just relations between those affected and, in a society such as ours where media are so all-pervasive, this can require forms of censorship.

This may even be true in matters of political censorship. In order to protect those who were persecuted by the Nazis and in order to prevent a resurgence of Nazism, the West German government has had legislation forbidding the use of various Nazi symbols. In terms of being just to the parties concerned I would say that this has been a wise move. Of course, it goes without saying that we must be extremely careful about any political restrictions because they can so easily lead to authoritarian states and because political freedom of expression is essential to any responsible politics. Nevertheless, in this area too, it must be justice and not abstract universal rights that provides the guide.

Abortion

The question of abortion poses similar problems. If we believe that the fetus has a right to life, which I do, then we still face a multitude of questions.[12] A human right to life is not absolute because, for example, soldiers can legitimately be asked to risk their lives in a just war. One person may need a kidney transplant to survive but we would not, I think, feel comfortable in *forcing* someone else to donate one of their own kidneys. Life itself is not an absolute but it must be weighed, along with everything else, in the scales of justice.

The same cautions must be made about a woman's right to control her body. This is an important freedom to be protected and there must be very important grounds for overriding it, for if a person cannot decide about their own body, they are usually not free to decide much else. But there are others who are also involved in a decision about abortion – the father, the doctors, the people who will pay for it and, most vitally, the fetus itself.

Because abortion involves at least the fetus and the mother, that is, more than one human life, it cannot be treated as only a matter of personal choice. Governments have a responsibility here as much as they would in the matter of owning slaves, which cannot be a matter of personal choice either. This position is not one of 'imposing morality' on other people, it is merely trying to ensure that human life is treated justly. Governments are required, as much as they can, to establish just relations between the parties involved in a decision about abortion. They must weigh the rights of the mother and the fetus and, as the most basic right of the fetus, the right to life, is at stake, there must be weighty grounds on the side of the mother if an abortion is to take place.

It is not my intention here to detail what legislation there should be on abortion, or on pornography. I am merely trying to suggest how we should approach such problems. Nevertheless our discussion so far suggests one thing about abortion. It suggests that a decision about abortion should, if possible, not be solely a personal decision or even a medical decision. It should be a judicial decision based on personal and medical grounds.[13]

Political Consequences

So far we have looked at pornography and abortion somewhat in isolation, focussing only on the question of whether either of them provides grounds for legal control. But there are many other things which must enter into such decisions. One of them is what the actual consequences of any legislative action might be. For example, does restricting abortions make any difference to the number of abortions carried out or does it merely replace legal with illegal abortions? I am not saying that this is the case, but this is a central question. Similarly, would strict legislation against pornography merely drive it underground and further into the hands of organised crime? What about cannabis, prostitution or gambling? Would legislation actually stop them or, like the 1920's prohibition of alcohol in the U.S., would it merely drive them into association with other criminal activities and make the situation worse? Where there is no consensus in society that something is wrong, then government action forbidding that something always has the adverse consequence, of disrespect for and flouting of the law.

We could respond to the persistence of such activities by cracking down with stronger penalties, more police and severe enforcement. But this too can bring awful consequences in its wake in the form of a controlled society or a police state, and other crimes can go uninvestigated and unpunished. These are important questions for justice precisely because the purpose of the law is *not* to enforce moral behaviour regardless of the consequences. Governments have to deal justly not with some abstract ideal realm but with the concrete society with all its trends and opinions, that they actually govern. This may well mean that the legal standards for activities such as abortion or prostitution will be less than a 'moral' requirement, simply because a more strict limit is unenforceable, or enforceable only with dire consequences.

Nor should we concentrate just on legislation which allows and forbids. We must also consider the political role of encouraging and enabling just actions. Forbidding the portrayal of violence against women will, in the long run, do little to stop that violence unless men develop new attitudes towards women. Indeed, many abortions come about because men refuse to accept responsibility for a child and demand that an, often unwilling, woman have an abortion or face desertion. This calls for evangelism and Christian teaching, but it also calls for government action which elevates and protects the status of women. Stronger legislation against abortion would not stop abortion unless various causes of abortion are addressed. This means changing the widespread social attitudes that see children as a hindrance to a self-fulfilled life. It also means making it possible for women to be able to bring up in a healthy way the children to whom they have given birth. This requires helping single women and poor women who cannot afford another child. This requires governmental action, and it is also a major challenge to churches and to Christians to share their goods.

Saying that 'societies only change when enough individuals' hearts change' is, in most of its forms, just not true because it neglects the fact that politics and law and economics are themselves things under God and require action in their own right. But this saying does point to an important truth. This is the truth that politics and legislation can, in the long run, accomplish little on their own. If laws that are passed are in opposition to the commitments, hearts and lives of the population at large then those laws will eventually be swept away or they must be enforced by a police state. Christian politics requires Christian evangelism and discipleship, and Christian patience.

SUMMARY

In this chapter I have tried to outline some ways of moving from the political examples and teaching of the Bible to action in the modern world. The core commandments – to love God with all our heart, mind, soul and strength and to love our neighbours as ourselves – are expressed in a more detailed way in the Ten Commandments. These commandments are, in turn, worked out in all the various dimensions of the life of Israel in the books of Leviticus, Numbers and Deuteronomy. The prophets point back to them and show their implications for the age in which they live. Jesus interprets the law by pointing to the core and the intent which it expresses and he tells his disciples to live out that intent in new ways.

We too must live out that law in our own situation. Our guide must not be any of the idols of the modern age but it must be the law of God, which shows what love means. At the same time we must take history and change, human responsibility and human freedom, seriously. We must respond to new situations and work out God's commandments in the actual settings where we live.

In order to act in this world, we must know what this world is like and how it works. This requires us to develop a Christian analysis of societies. Two key elements of such an analysis are (a) the religious nature of human beings, who will always seek to serve either God or idols in all that they do, and (b) the permanence of God's created ordinances which always restrain the effects of human sin and help keep all people on the track of obedience and service.

Although I have tried to show the implications of such an analysis for understanding political parties and 'moral' questions, it is not enough on its own to deal with many of the questions that face us. Consequently, in the next two chapters, when we look at the issues of the welfare state and nuclear arms, I will try

to expand on this analysis and show its implications. In doing so
I will introduce some further elements of any Christian analysis,
especially the nature of stewardship, the status of the poor,
'realism' and 'idealism' in international relations, and views of
war.

5: Economics and the Welfare State

IDOLATRY AND ECONOMICS

Our Economic Problems

Most political discussions today are about economics. In fact party political platforms are composed almost entirely of economic matters. Most parties have no positions on anything else: items such as capital punishment are left to a 'free vote'. Only the deadly urgency of the nuclear arms race has managed to squeeze in alongside economics as a matter of party debate. A cursory glance at the newspaper seems to demonstrate that money makes the world go around.

Despite the preoccupation with economic questions, such questions appear to be more and more intractable.[1] The West has been mired in recession with the hitherto unthinkable combination of both inflation and unemployment. Even the prospect of a mild economic upturn holds out little hope for the majority of the unemployed, who seem condemned to a life of poverty and social rejection. Very few people hold out any hope for long term economic growth. The period of sustained growth in the fifties and sixties now seems like a golden past, an aberration which will not be repeated.

The communist countries are in even worse shape. The Soviet Union appears to have ended its remarkable decades-long economic growth and is mired in inefficiency and a declining infrastructure. The Russian satellites are generally in bad shape, especially Poland, which is deeply in debt to western banks.

The 'third world' remains poor and, for most, the long heralded economic 'take-off' seems a cruel hoax perpetrated by rapacious western countries. The shock of the OPEC oil price rises devastated third world economies, driving them further into debt, so that most of them must use all their foreign exchange merely to make interest payments on their debts. When these countries ask for a restructuring of world trade, the communist bloc blames the West, while the West offers only promises and complains that it can't do anything until its own economy is back in shape.

The futurologists and social scientists have started becoming apocalyptic just at the time that many Christians have given up on visions of the end of the world. The Club of Rome, acting as a sort of world elite think tank, has suggested that the end of our human world will be sometime in the next century unless we repent and change our ways.

Economics as Salvation

This combination of a fixation on economics coupled with economic impotence seems to bear the symptoms of idolatry. This is confirmed if we examine our situation more closely. It is not too much to say that in our society a person's worth is thought to be determined by the value of their possessions. We believe that the aim of life is to have more TV's, radios, washers, cars. We are bombarded by advertising with the message that material things will make us happy. Our government's project, insofar as it has one, is to increase economic growth, which means, quite simply, to have more things. In the old bible of revisionist socialism, *The Future of Socialism*, Anthony Crosland argued that higher growth rates were needed to finance more welfare. Similarly while Mrs. Thatcher argues that 'The mission of this government is far more than the promotion of economic progress . . .' yet this remains her government's central concern.[2]

The creed of our society is a confession that peace, security and happiness (all the benefits of salvation) will come about sometime in the future if only we can produce more. Despite their denunciation of capitalist materialism, the creed of Marxists is, quite simply, that when we produce so much that everyone has enough, then there will be nothing to fight about anymore. Everyone can satisfy their needs and the government will 'wither away' because it has nothing left to do. A life of human freedom and free self-expression will then begin. Many Christians have criticised this Marxist pseudo-faith, but fewer have pointed out that, on this point at least, capitalism and communism are at one. They both believe that the purpose of political life is to ensure and allow the creation of more things and that this creation will solve our problems, at least those that can be solved politically.

As John Kenneth Galbraith has pointed out, 'A rising standard of living has the aspect of a *faith* in our culture'.[3] It is a faith by which we live – it is our hope for the future. One of the remarkable facts about our society is how future-oriented it is. What is good is always in the future. Harold MacMillan's 'you never had it so good' is the exception that proves the rule. We live for tomorrow, it will happen tomorrow, we can have it tomorrow. Our society continues because we believe it will be different tomorrow. If we were all told that where we are now and what we have now is all there's going to be, it is doubtful if our social structure could survive the outrage. We put up with things now because a new age will come, maybe.

The most influential English economist of this century, John Maynard Keynes, saw this with his customary clarity. In 1930 he wrote 'For at least another hundred years we must pretend to ourselves and to everyone that fair is foul and foul is fair; for foul is useful and fair is not. Avarice and usury and precaution must be our gods for a little longer still. For only they can lead us out of the tunnel of economic necessity into daylight'.[4] Keynes' reference to 'gods' was rhetorical, but he spoke more than he knew. We accept avarice and we believe it will save us. We will go beyond necessity and reach the realm of freedom through our economic gods.

But, as we try to create a society in the image of these gods, they bind us and trap us. Whatever we do becomes conformed to our idol. As Galbraith points out:

> If we continue to believe that the goals of the industrial system – the expansion of output, the companion increase in consumption, technological advance, the public images that sustain it – are coordinate with life, then all of our lives will be in service of these goals. What is consistent with these ends we shall have or be allowed; all else will be off limits. Our wants will be managed in accordance with the needs of the industrial system; the policies of the state will be subject to similar influence; education will be adapted to industrial need; the disciplines required by the industrial system will be the conventional morality of the community. All other goals will be made to seem precious, unimportant or antisocial. We will be bound to the ends of the industrial system.[5]

Economic Impotence

What is remarkable about this fixation with economic growth, and part of what reveals it as an idol, is that it does not bring the fulfilment that is claimed for it.[6] Obviously if a person does not have enough to eat then having more will radically improve their wellbeing. The same is true for other basic needs that can be gained with money, such as clothing, and shelter. However, at the income levels of most inhabitants of the West (i.e. excluding those on the dole), an increase in income does not seem to relate at all to an increase in wellbeing.

The surveys which have been done on 'subjective' qualities of life (i.e. asking people how satisfied with their life they are) show results which are markedly in contrast to our dominant social myths. One survey of eight North Atlantic countries found that Canada, with the highest output per capita of the group, ranked fourth in percent of satisfied people. The Republic of Ireland, on the other hand, ranked last of the group in output per capita, but was second highest in satisfied people. In a similar vein an American sociologist examined opinion polls since World War II which dealt with the question of whether people were happy. Despite the fact that real income more than doubled in this period, he found *no change at all* in the percentage of people who described themselves as 'happy'.[7]

While the sociologists go about demonstrating that it does not profit us to gain the world and lose our own soul, we see all sorts of ill effects coming along with our pattern of economic growth. Vital raw materials and energy reserves are being used up at a rapid rate, the number of species of plants and animals in the world is decreasing, the ecosystem of the oceans is threatened. There is increasing psychological stress and mental illness, an increase in crime and divorce (which correlates well with economic growth) and general alienation, especially of teenagers. With this growth we have increasing shortages, especially of time but also of opportunities for intimacy and tenderness. Nor, while unemployment rises to 12.3% (mid-1983), has economic growth in recent years come close to solving our economic problems. Meanwhile the inequalities between rich and poor grow greater and, on a world scale, the absolute number of the poor has been increasing. These are not just problems caused by the recession of the last five years, although that recession has exacerbated them. These are basic structural problems with our life itself. An upturn in economic growth will adjust the numbers a little, but it will not overcome these problems; indeed in many cases (such as with shortages of raw materials) it will make the problems worse.

In his important book, *The Social Limits to Growth*, the late Fred Hirsch suggested at least two reasons why these problems will get worse.[8] One is the importance of what he calls 'positional goods', things which only have value as long as a few people have them. If only a few people can afford to go to the beach, then the beach is worth going to. But, because the beach is worth going to then more people want more money so they can go to the beach. If everybody gets enough money to go to the beach, then everybody goes. The end result is that the beach is crowded and is no fun any more! Hirsch says that many of the things we value are like a trip to the beach. Everybody can't have them at once. This is a problem which no amount of 'wealth' can alter.

The other reason Hirsch suggests is that there is a conflict between the patterns of life required to increase economic growth and the patterns of life which make for a healthy community. We need discipline, self-control, honesty and good work habits in order to increase *production*. But, in order to *consume* all the things we have produced, we need leisure, continual borrowing, greed, wastefulness and self-interest. These two sets of traits are in basic conflict with one another. Furthermore, the values we need in order to increase consumption are hardly the ones that go into making solid marriages, families, schools, universities, churches, politics, or work places. For both of these reasons, Hirsch suggests that our economic rat race is more like the race of mice running forever in a wheel and never getting anywhere.

THE WELFARE STATE

The History of the Welfare State

The welfare state as we know it in the United Kingdom and in western Europe (as well as, to a lesser extent, in North America and Australasia) is a relatively recent phenomenon. Its beginnings lay in attempts to combat the great depression of the thirties. In the United Kingdom its chief architects were William Beveridge and John Maynard Keynes.

In 1944 Sir William Beveridge produced a government report entitled *Social Insurance and Allied Services*. Its basic theme was 'freedom from want', a term borrowed from United States President Roosevelt's famous 'four freedoms' speech of 1941. The idea was that the state could and should provide a 'safety net', a minimum standard of living for everyone. Social security was the first step on this path to the welfare state. It was followed by similar proposals in the areas of housing and health (the National Health Service).

Meanwhile the implications of Keynes' *The General Theory of Employment, Interest and Money*, published in 1936, were being understood in government circles. Put simply (too simply), Keynes said that when there was oversaving and underconsumption (people saving rather than spending money or else not having enough to spend) in the economy then the government could and should get and keep the economy growing by spending money itself. Governments could borrow money in order to do so. Then, in better economic times, the government could recoup additional income from taxes and, over the long term, maintain something like a balanced budget, spending only as much as it took in. Thus the government could maintain relatively constant demand in the economy and could produce continuing economic growth. Another means by which this oversaving could be tackled was redistribution of income – taking from the rich and giving to the poor. Lower income people actually spend – have to spend – their money rather than save it, so such a redistribution of income will itself lead to increased spending and increased economic activity.

Beveridgean guarantees and Keynesian economic policy fit hand in glove and it seemed that this combination would solve the economic problems of the West. Government could redistribute income and have not only social but also solid economic grounds for doing so. They could spend on job creation and social security and, by doing so, they could help private enterprise and the overall economy. Good social goals were at the same time good economic policies. It seemed as though governments could have the rate of economic growth they wanted, the level of employment they wished to reach, and the income distribution that they desired. All that was required was 'fine tuning' the economy.

The promise seemed to be so great that Beveridgean and Keynesian policies were followed throughout the capitalist world. Sweden was first off the mark but other nations followed rapidly in its path. Welfare state policies became the platform of nearly all political parties, whether they described themselves as conservative or socialist, liberal or christian democrat. All political differences seemed to be relatively minor ones within the basic overall acceptance of the framework of the welfare state. Parties became more and more like one another and, because of their similarities, were reduced to emphasising 'leadership' and 'ability' as their gifts to the electorate, without needing to specify leadership or ability at what and why. Some even spoke of the 'end of ideology': political problems had gone, only administrative ones remained. Some countries planned more, some less. Some countries had self-proclaimed socialist or conservative governments. But all followed the same basic policies.

These policies also had a feature not common to economic prescriptions – they worked! Between World War II and 1967, unemployment in Britain averaged $1^1/2\%$. There was a long period of sustained economic growth, higher in Europe than in the United Kingdom, but present even here. The future looked rosy.

Only further time was needed to usher in a new, wealthy, just society.

The Crisis of the Welfare State

But the dream did not last, as no dream can that believes that security will be achieved by technical measures. The stress on material abundance and on virtually a *right* to material abundance led every group, weak or strong, to strive to acquire a bigger 'slice of the pie'. After 1963 wages were pushed up because of low unemployment. Profit levels began to decrease, slowly but constantly. When OPEC raised the price of oil in 1973, it hit economies which had already for a decade witnessed slowly declining profits and rates of investment. The oil price rise led to balance of payment problems as non-OPEC countries spent more abroad for oil than they took in at home for their exports. The result was a contraction of world trade and a slowdown in economic growth. Governments reacted with the by now traditional solution of trying to spend their way out of trouble, but this time it didn't work. Both inflation and unemployment continued to rise, a combination formerly thought to be impossible.

The combination of economic stagnation, inflation and unemployment ('stagflation') is still where we are now, although some of the numbers, especially on inflation, are starting to look brighter. This combination is bad enough at any time, but it is lethal for the welfare state, because it makes directly contradictory demands on the government. In bad economic times fewer taxes come in, and so governments have fewer and fewer resources at their disposal. But, because of those same bad economic times, the needs which governments must meet are much greater – more people are unemployed, more people are ill, more companies need bail-outs. Governments take in less and need to spend more. The result is larger and larger budget deficits.

This process also acts like a trap, for almost every economic policy seems only to make matters worse. If governments spend less then income and consumption in the economy go down, and so the economy suffers further and, in turn, government revenues decline further. If the government spends more then inflation and interest rates shoot up, industrial investment and home building decline, and government revenues decline again. The welfare state seems locked in a downward spiral where anything it does makes the situation deteriorate. In the United Kingdom, the situation would be even worse if it were not for the revenues brought in by North Sea oil, but these too will decline shortly.

Governments generally do not know what to do in this situation.

The more left-wing parties stress the importance of fighting unemployment and they pay the price for it in inflation (which also hurts the poor most). The more right-wing parties stress the importance of fighting inflation and they pay the price for it in unemployment and bankruptcy – or rather, their citizens pay the price. The older solutions do not appear to work and so governments are resorting to more extreme policies. Mrs Thatcher and Ronald Reagan are spending by trying to dismantle the welfare state itself, by trying to return to the older days of smaller government and the 'forces of the market'. The Labour party, or a large part of it, seems to have decided that the old social-democratic, mixed-economy, welfare state style of socialism won't work any more and is moving toward a more full-blooded central-ised state socialism. The Liberal/Social-Democratic Alliance tries to avoid 'extremism' but then seems to end up with business-as-usual welfare policies, which are precisely what seem to be unten-able right now.

I have stressed the international rather than the national dimensions of the crisis of the welfare state. This is because I want to emphasise the basic, *structural* and *spiritual* nature of the problems we face. Some countries have higher unemployment or inflation or economic growth, but basically we are all in the same boat (Japan is a different sort of country, but even there similar problems are now being felt). It is not just a case of blaming this or that party or tendency (or rather, it *is* a case of blaming them *all*). Instead, we need to radically examine our basic beliefs about economics and about what leads to a healthy life if we are to move in any healing direction.

To aid in this examination we will look in the next section at what the Scriptures tell us about economic life. But we must be aware, even as we do so, that there will be no magical solutions. We will have to work through a long, hard path of building and restoration. In fact it is improbable that we will, in the foreseeable future, retrieve the economic growth rates of the sixties. It is also doubtful whether we ought to. We should instead try to discover what it means to want, not *more*, but *enough*.[9]

ECONOMICS AS STEWARDSHIP

The Meaning of Stewardship

The word 'economics' is derived from the Greek *oikonomia*, which is usually translated in the Scriptures as 'stewardship'. The items we usually think of as economic questions are treated in the

Bible as 'stewardship' questions. To be an economist or to be economically productive is to be a good steward. But what does a good steward do?

Stewardship is an extremely broad term. We have already used it as one way of describing the 'cultural mandate'. A steward is someone who is appointed by the owner of property to manage the affairs of the household. The steward typically made sure that the servants were well looked after, or at least were obedient (only wealthy households could have stewards). They also made sure that the animals were healthy, the crops were harvested and planted properly, the children were behaving, and that investments were made wisely. Such stewards were common illustrations in Jesus' parables: he used them as examples, both good and bad ones, to the disciples of how they should behave as citizens of the Kingdom of God (cf. Luke 12:35–48; 16:1–13; 19:11–27).

The steward is one whom the master appoints to stand in his stead, to look after affairs in the way the master wants, and who will give account to the master of what he or she has done. This is why stewardship is one way of describing the task of humankind on the earth. People are God's stewards, standing in God's stead. We do not own the earth, God does. We are to manage it as good stewards who seek to do our master's will and who will give an accounting of our stewardship on the last day. In this vein, Jesus says to Peter 'Who then is the faithful and wise steward, whom his master will set over his household, to give them their portion of food at the proper time? Blessed is that servant whom his master when he comes will find him so doing.' (Luke 12:42–43)

For this reason the 'cultural mandate' should not be understood as a licence for humankind to dominate the earth. We should not read the words about 'subduing', 'conquering', 'filling', and 'having dominion' over the earth as though they were licences for unbridled exploitation. As we have seen, there are enough examples in the Scriptures of caring for the earth in its own right. The land must be protected, it must be honoured, trees and waters must be protected. The cultural mandate calls us to steward the earth like a good and healthy household. The Christian faith has been criticised for licensing the domination of nature, a domination which has resulted in the resource depletion, pollution and ugliness that desecrates much of the world. But this concept of Christianity is miles apart from the biblical teaching of filling and caring for the creation.

Perhaps it could be argued that what the Bible says is one thing, but that what Christians actually have taught and done is entirely another matter. This argument must be taken very seriously indeed for here we are not concerned with defending this original integrity of the Christian faith but with understanding our own history and situation. Yet even in terms of history this critique of Christian faith is wide of the mark. The theme of the domination of nature appears clearly in the seventeenth century, particularly in such Stoically inclined figures as Francis Bacon. The increasing exploitation of nature since the eighteenth century coincides with the decline of Christianity as a formative force in the West. The economic ideologies which have enshrined such exploitation came into their own in the industrial revolution, just at the time that Christian social teaching became more out-of-date and irrelevant. The twentieth century, the great age of the rape of the natural world, is also the great age of secularity. Rather than looking for the ideological roots of our present exploitation in the Christian faith, one might better look to humanism, whose creed 'Man is the measure of all things' has produced the greatest disjuncture between the human world and the natural world.

Given that our economic activity is to be the loving stewardship of the earth and all that is in it, we must have a clearer idea of what is required by that stewardship. First, it must be said that we are the stewards not only of natural things like land, soil, trees, oceans and minerals. We are the stewards of all things – including time, energy, health, organisation, family life, work styles, buildings – everything that exists in human life. Secondly, to steward all these things is to treat them in the way that God calls us to treat them, being careful to attend to all the ways in which we can express love – through justice, through beauty, through preservation, through use, through faithfulness. To steward something is first of all to be aware of its place in God's creation, to be sensitive to all the ways it can be hurt and to all the ways it can bring benefits to others, and then to preserve it and cause it to be 'fruitful' – to care for it so that what is good is preserved and to use it so that it brings blessing to other things. This is what stewardship is and, therefore, this is what proper economics is.

Such stewardship can be illustrated through the actions of a family. Let us suppose that the husband has a job outside the home, that the wife focusses her work inside the home, and that the husband is offered a new job at higher pay a few hundred miles away. If the family is Christianly responsible then their decision about the job should go something like this. All the family, parents and children, will get together to talk about what will be lost and what will be gained, for them and for others, by taking or not taking the new job.

On the 'loss side' might be such things as: a disruption of the kids' schooling and friendships and neighbourhood; separation from a church community; separation of the wife from her friends and ties; separation from the extended family, grandparents, aunts, uncles, and cousins; leaving a known and happy work situation; depriving a company of a valuable employee; the physical and emotional disruption of the move itself. This list could, of course, be multiplied endlessly but this is enough to point out the *costs* possibly connected with the move.

On the 'gain' or 'benefit' side may be: more money (not to be sniffed at); more challenging work; work which is of better service to the community; the possibility of joining or helping develop a new church community; moving closer to the extended family; widening circles of friendship, and so on. These are some of the possible gains from such a move.

The family should consider all of these effects and try to determine whether any injustice will be done to somebody by moving (justice), whether any promises will be broken by moving (unfaithfulness), and then, if neither of these is the case, the family will weigh the benefits and losses of the proposed move and decide whether overall it is a good thing to do.

In trying to make a decision this way the family is engaging in the activity that the Bible calls stewardship. It is real *economic* activity. Economics should not be understood as referring only to what we now call 'economic' things, such as money, jobs, interest rates, or buying and selling. Real economics is an activity that tries to deal with *everything* in a *stewardly* way. This is true for families, for individuals, for companies, for churches, for governments. All of these must be stewardly in their activities.

The Lack of Stewardship in Economic Life

This process of stewardship can be contrasted with the activities which we now usually (mis)call economics. Consider how our corporations, whether good or bad, make and carry out their decisions, or, even, consider how the man in the family, assuming he's an executive, usually makes decisions for the company for which he works. Let us say a decision is being made whether or not to develop facilities in a Scottish town as a base for North Sea oil exploration. Throughout the life of the project, as it opens, produces and then (inevitably) closes down, there are a whole variety of possible benefits and costs. We can list some of these:

Possible Benefits	*Possible Costs*
– Producing needed materials	– Providing poor jobs
– Providing jobs	– Using up raw materials

- Providing good jobs
- Income for families
- Payments of taxes for government services
- Providing return on investment
- Profits for further investment
- Keeping the town alive – making possibilities to establish churches, schools and sports teams

- Diversion of capital from other possible projects
- Pollution
- Causing dislocation of the town when the oil is gone, disrupting neighbourhoods, families, schools, churches
- Driving up local prices so that long-time residents become relatively poorer
- Unemployment when the project ends

Again, these lists could be extended, both on the positive and the negative side. My point is that an *economic* (stewardly) act is one that recognises and tries to weigh all these effects in reaching a decision.

But we (as companies or, perhaps, even as families) don't usually make economic decisions this way. Companies look only at a few of the costs and benefits. The benefits emphasised inside the company are income and profits, and the ones emphasised by the company to the public at large are jobs and wages. The costs emphasised internally are payments which must be made for wages, rent, raw materials, cleaning up pollution and borrowing money. Then if *these particular benefits* are greater than *these particular costs*, the company proceeds with the project, if it can.

But, as we can see from this list, it is quite possible that *these* benefits can be greater than *these* costs even though the *overall costs* may be much greater than the benefits. We are continually neglecting all sorts of costs in our present economic decision making. Instead of being really economic (stewardly) in our dealing with all things we focus on *certain* things, usually ones which have a price tag, and make a decision on their basis only. Consequently we can end up, and clearly we do end up, consistently making decisions that are really *uneconomic*, decisions that consistently have greater real costs than benefits, decisions that make us poorer as people while maintaining the illusion that we are 'growing' economically. The country can fall apart even if the economic indicators look good.

These other costs should not be treated merely as amounts in pounds and pence that can be paid for, for such a treatment implies that they are worth only whatever someone is willing to pay for them. But clearly, poor people would be willing to pay much less than rich people for something, for the simple reason that they don't have much to pay with. Hence assigning a value in pounds overemphasises the views of those who are wealthy. Assigning items like family disruption a 'market value' completely neglects the relative incomes of the different sorts of people who might be affected.

Even though we really can't assign amounts in pounds, it can still be a useful exercise to ask whether, if these costs (and the additional benefits) were given monetary amounts and charged (or credited) to the company, it would still want to go ahead with the project. If it did not want to go ahead then we would have a clear indication that the project is, in a real sense, an uneconomic one. Yet, despite this fact, we continue to go ahead with such projects without knowing or dealing with their real costs.

It is not that such a company, or its executives, is especially wicked (although it might be). It usually doesn't matter whether such executives (or union leaders) are bad people or good people: they are intrinsically no better or worse than the rest of us, although the effects of what they do are more widespread. The problem is that we have structured our economics so that many real costs and benefits are never dealt with.

In emphasising stewardship, I am not offering a 'moral' critique of economics. Nor am I saying that 'ethical' questions must be considered *alongside* 'economic' questions, nor that 'social' questions should be considered *alongside* 'economic' questions. I am saying that these costs and benefits are themselves *actual*, *real*, *concrete*, *intrinsic*, *economic* questions. I am saying that to be anything other than a steward is uneconomic, wasteful, and inefficient. We should not try to add 'Christian ethics' to economics. Instead we should strive for a *Christianly inspired economics itself*; one which is rooted in the biblical view of stewardship.

THE WELFARE STATE IN LIGHT OF STEWARDSHIP

The Mirage of Economic Growth

We have seen that our society is committed to economic growth. But there is nothing wrong with growth. We should always desire that what is truly economic should continue to grow. Societies are made to grow – to grow in justice, in stewardship, in care for one another, in needed goods, in fulfilling work, in humane environments. We should not be opposed to real economic growth.

But what we now call 'growth' is often anything but truly economic. Our usual indicator of economic growth is the Gross National Product (GNP) which is the gross sum in pounds of all the goods we produce and all the services we provide involving money. The GNP does *not* measure *all* goods and services but only those that involve money. This measure is like the company in our example of oil exploration. It focusses on a particular range of costs and benefits as if they were the only ones or, at least, the only important ones. But, despite this narrow focus, our government's economic policies are geared toward making this GNP rise, with little regard for how the GNP actually relates to substantive human wellbeing.

The point is not that the GNP should not rise. It is that such a rise itself indicates nothing about human wellbeing. Many things add to our GNP. Smoking and other forms of pollution do, both in consumption and in the medical services which must follow. Marital breakdown and divorce are good for the GNP because people no longer share TV's or beds and need to buy one each. Shift work is good for the GNP, and not bad for marital breakdown either. Eating out is good for the GNP. Eating at home is not.

Clearly the relation between GNP and human wellbeing is not a simple one. If you grow your own food, or make your own clothing, or chop your own wood, or fix up your own dwelling, then very little enters the GNP figures. If you pay someone else to do these things for you, then the GNP goes up. Raising children and doing housework does not enter the GNP, but if it is contracted out then it does. Putting Granny in a home helps the GNP, keeping her at home does not. Merely by the book-keeping device of including the household sector in the GNP we could raise it by 30–60%.

Unpaid voluntary work, such as visiting hospitals or old people does not enter the GNP, but paying social workers to do exactly the same task does. Seeking advice from a friend doesn't help the GNP, seeking the same advice from a psychologist does. The GNP does not record the sum of human economic activities, but only those which are done for money. Consequently when our economic indicators rise we don't know if we are doing more or doing less, we only know that we are doing more of it for money.

Because of the way we collect economic statistics, relevant figures are not available, but it seems to be true that much of our 'economic growth' is not adding new goods and services but merely shifting things away from unpaid, domestic or voluntary activity and into paid activity. This shift is itself neither right nor wrong, but it is certainly wrong to call it growth without further question in that it can be merely a shifting around of activities, or even represent a breakdown of community and neighbourhood spirit, a weakening of family ties, and the increased commercialisation of life.

This type of confusion pervades our economic categories them-selves. If the local fish and chip shop buys an oven, economists call it 'investment'. If a family buys the same oven, economists call it 'consumption'. Yet the same output is produced. And we are often told to cut down on 'consumption' in order to maintain 'investment' levels! Much of today's economic discourse operates in its own closed world, sealed off from real contact with the things which actually make life worth living.

Government 'Two-Track' Policies

Government 'economic' policy is concentrated in that fairly narrow range of economic activities which involve money. Any non-monied economic activities are treated as separate or 'private'. Government's goal is to increase the GNP without too high a cost in inflation and, until recently, in unemployment. These are the features that cabinet ministers with 'economic' port-folios (the Chancellor of the Exchequer, Chief Secretary to the Treasury, Industry and Trade) are supposed to look after. These ministries are the 'higher' cabinet posts, the plum jobs, because this type of economics is thought to be the highest goal of government.

But this process of boosting 'economic' growth ignores many of the real costs and benefits that we outlined earlier. Families can be disrupted, unemployment can lead to loss of meaning, to crime, to alcoholism, even to suicide. People can find themselves lonelier and their work ever more crippling and deadening. For a long time governments ignored these effects but, to its eternal credit, the welfare state has been an attempt to address these matters, usually under the heading of 'social policy'. So we have had social security plans, the National Health Service, job retraining programmes, and so on. We now have government agencies whose job it is to pick up the 'hidden costs', the ignored effects, of our dealing with economic matters.

The combined result is a 'two-track' government approach.[10] One track is 'economic policy', which is to boost 'economic growth' and, if possible, to keep inflation and unemployment in check. The other track is 'social policy' to deal with all the things neglected by the 'economic policy'. The 'economic policy' is supposed to produce enough wealth so that government can afford a decent 'social policy'. Typically, right wing governments call themselves 'realists' and emphasise 'economic' policy by saying that, in the long run, this is the only way to afford the 'social' programmes. Left wing governments emphasise 'social policy' and, of late, are quite fuzzy on 'economic policy'.

The overall pattern is that real economic (stewardly) activities are artificially divided in two. Some costs and benefits are separated out as 'economic', and the others are left as 'social'. Efforts are then made to boost the 'economic' in order to get taxes to pay for the 'social'. The process is like a merry-go-round, for as the 'economic' gains increase (if they do increase) so do the 'social' costs, and so the economic must increase even more, and thus the spiral repeats itself.

One aspect of the crisis of the welfare state is that the 'economic' benefits have not kept pace with the 'social' costs. Governments do not have enough revenue to deal with 'social' needs. The difference between these gains and losses is roughly indicated by ballooning government budget deficits. These deficits are an indication that for several years our real stewardly costs have been greater than the benefits. During the time of economic growth we have been getting in a real sense poorer and poorer. We produce more commodities yet our social fabric unravels. We have been able to go through the longest period of sustained 'economic growth' in human history and yet have found ourselves in an economic crisis at the end of it. Clearly, we have not been accumulating real wealth.

Towards Stewardship

We should emphasise neither 'economic policy' nor 'social policy' at the expense of the other, for they are both essential parts of stewardship. We cannot select either 'realist' economics or 'compassionate' economics, for, if realism is to be true to the real human world then it must be compassionate and, if compassion is to be more than pious exhortation, then it must be realistic. Instead we must avoid the 'two track' framework altogether and try to make our corporate, family, individual and government decisions ones which are stewardly from the word go. We must make decisions about starting factories, developing new technologies, moving families, buying food, and adjusting taxes on the basis of their effects on unemployment, family life, production of genuinely needed things and gentleness to the environment as well as on their effects on incomes, profits and inflation. Right from the beginning we must be stewards and weigh the options before us.

There are no predetermined answers in such a process. Such a weighing of options cannot be reduced to flow charts on econometricians' print outs. Like everything else done in God's world it is always an act of responsibility. Economic acts must be acts of service designed to bring health and wellbeing to our neighbours.

Anything else will be not just unethical or uncaring, it will also be wasteful, inefficient, unstewardly, *uneconomic*. While no ethical theory (or theological theory for that matter) can *dictate* what will be a stewardly decision in any given instance, yet we can learn about priorities in costs and benefits. The major economic priority in the Scriptures is the priority of the poor, and it is to this that we shall now turn our attention.

THE POOR

The Biblical Emphasis on the Poor

In careful exegesis and pointed application the theologians of liberation have shown the centrality of the poor, and not just the spiritually poor, in the gospel message. Once we become aware of this it calls us from every page. Most churches in the country repeat the words of the *Magnificat* every Sunday:

'He has put down the mighty from their thrones,
and exalted those of low degree;
He has filled the hungry with good things,
and the rich He has sent empty away.' (Luke 1:52–53)

But we fail to see what Mary saw about the child in her womb. We spiritualise these words. Of course they do also mean the rich in conceit and the poor in spirit, but they mean more than this.

The poor in Scripture include those who are poor in many ways.[11] The poor are coupled with the hungry, the homeless, the stranger, the widow, the orphan, the sick, the meek, the oppressed, the prisoners, the blind and those who are bowed down (Ps. 10; Ps. 146). It is certainly true that an orphan or a widow is often in dire financial straits, especially in our society where they comprise most of the poor. But they also suffer from loneliness, isolation and lack of warmth and stability – things not related solely to financial conditions. The command to care for the poor is the command to care for all those who are suffering and sorrowing. We may say that in Scripture *the poor are those who lack the social, economic, political, or spiritual resources to fulfil God's calling for their lives*. Yet, while it is clear that poverty is more than money, lack of food, shelter, clothing, work and money are a large part of it. This is especially true today, for in our society more and more things are available only for money. Access to the law, health, leisure and privacy is becoming as dependent on income as is food and clothing.

In the law, God continually commands Israel to care for the fatherless, the widow and the sojourner (Exod. 22:21–24; Lev. 19:15; Deut. 1:7; 10:17–18). It was God who brought Israel itself out of bondage and who always defends the poor and needy (Exod. 6:5–7; 20:2; Deut. 5:6; 10:17–18; 26:5–8).

These commands are also the continual refrain of the prophets. Isaiah calls Israel to seek justice and righteousness – specifically in caring for the fatherless, the widow and the poor (Isa. 1:21:26). The psalmist praises the Lord,

> who executes justice for the oppressed; who gives food to the hungry. The Lord sets the prisoners free; the Lord opens the eyes of the blind (Ps. 146:7–8).

The other side of these injunctions is condemnation of those who oppress the poor, including those who do not go to their aid. Amos denounces those 'who oppress the poor, who crush the needy' (Amos 4:1), while Isaiah condemns those who 'turn aside the needy from justice' (Isa. 10:1–4; see also Mark 12:40).

Jesus announces his own ministry in the words of Isaiah 61:1–2.

> The Spirit of the Lord is upon me, because he has anointed me to preach good news to the poor. He has sent me to proclaim release to the captives and recovering of sight to the blind, to set at liberty those who are oppressed. (Luke 4:18–19)

These words must not be 'spiritualised'. We know that Jesus heals the physically sick and the blind, feeds the hungry, and says

> I was hungry and you gave me food, I was thirsty and you gave me to drink, . . . I was naked and you clothed me, . . . Truly, I say to you, as you did it to one of the least of these my brethren, you did it to me (Matt. 25:35–40).

The apostle James is adamant on this score. 'Has not God chosen those who are poor in the world to be rich in faith and heirs of the kingdom . . . ?' (James 2:1–3). It would be hard to overestimate the continual stress throughout the Scriptures that God commands us continually and persistently to fight poverty and to care for the poor and needy.

We know that God's judgment, call to repentance, and promise of eternal life are given to rich and poor alike. Salvation, in all its dimensions, is by God's grace and not by human righteousness. But it is still crystal clear that the poor are singled out particularly for God's concern and protection. It is the poor, the hungry, and the oppressed to whom the Scriptures particularly refer. It is the rich who are singled out and condemned for their not caring for and, more particularly, their oppression of the poor. The rich are criticised because the economic arrangements which create their riches are also those which create poverty.

It is not that the poor are themselves personally righteous, but rather that God's righteousness requires justice for the poor. These texts do not mean that God is 'biased' towards the poor, for God requires equitable treatment for *all* people: 'You shall have one law for the sojourner and for the native; for I am the Lord your God. . . . You shall not be partial to the poor or defer to the great, but in righteousness shall you judge your neighbour.' (Lev. 19:15; Ex. 23:3).[12] Nevertheless God still singles out the poor because, almost by definition, the poor are those who are suffering injustice.

The Commands Concerning Poverty

The laws given to Israel concerning poverty cover both the personal and corporate aspects of their lives. Each Israelite was to be open-hearted and generous to the poor and needy (Deut. 15:7) and there was also a whole series of organised arrangements to remove poverty from the land. Loans *had* to be given to those in need, with no interest to be taken from a fellow Israelite. The gleanings of the fields and vineyards were to be left for the poor to take (Lev. 19:9–10). Every third year the tithes given to the Lord were collected in the towns so that the poor could come and be filled. Every seventh year all debts were forgiven and slaves were to be released with generous gifts (Deut. 15:1–18). Every fiftieth year was the year of Jubilee. In this year land which had been sold was to be freely returned to the seller (Lev. 25). As the land was to be equitably distributed among the Israelites when they first entered the promised land, this meant that no one could ultimately be separated from their means of livelihood. The major economic resources would continue to be divided equitably among the population (Lev. 25:6).

These laws give us a picture in a primitive agricultural setting of the sort of economic relations that God wishes for people. Their core message is that *Israel was to order its whole life together*, and in particular, its division of resources, *in such a way that nobody acquired too much and that those in need would continually be cared for*. 'Let there be no poor among you' (Deut. 15:4). Deuteronomy adds that 'the poor will never cease out of the land' (which Jesus quotes, Matt. 26:11) and so Israel must *permanently* 'open wide your hand to your brother' (15:11).

These laws also focus on God's *redemption*, for the year of Jubilee was to be proclaimed on the Day of Atonement. On this day Israel commemorated that they themselves were once poor, oppressed and aliens in the land of Egypt and that the Lord had delivered them. The Jubilee year is itself a memorial of God's deliverance. The fiftieth year and the seventh year were days to remember, to proclaim and to *re-enact* that deliverance; these years 'proclaimed the Lord's release' (Deut. 15:2; Lev. 25:9–10). Israelites were called, as God's covenant partners, to act towards one another as God had already acted and continues to act toward them: 'You shall remember that you were a slave in the land of Egypt, and the Lord your God redeemed you; therefore I command you this today' (Deut. 15:15). This is what Jesus alludes to in the Lord's prayer when he says 'forgive us our debts, as we also have forgiven our debtors' (Matt. 6:12). It is in terms of this picture of redemption that Jesus first announces his own ministry. At Nazareth he introduces himself in Isaiah's words as the one who will 'proclaim the acceptable year of the Lord' (Luke 4:19). Isaiah's words are in turn a reference to the proclamation of Jubilee (Lev. 25:10). Jesus is the One who will fulfil the year of Jubilee, the year of release, the year of the forgiveness of debts. *The picture given by the laws is one of redemption, liberation, and atonement expressed in all life, but here especially in economic life. Debts are forgiven, that which had been lost is redeemed, the slate is wiped clean and the poor are to have resources to begin again – we are not stretching the point if we say to be born again – economically.*

Jesus expressed this when he told us to give to those that ask of us, to feed the hungry and give drink to the thirsty. He cut to the core when he said 'blessed are you poor for yours is the Kingdom of God.' All other economic laws and practices, such as the early Church in Jerusalem pooling its goods (Acts 2:43f.) or Paul's collection for the Jerusalem Church (2 Cor. 8, 9), are attempts to express this love for the poor in differing times and circumstances.

Our Responsibility for the Poor

We are called to live out these commitments in our own lives. We cannot delegate our responsibility for the poor. We may not foist our own responsibilities off onto the state and say that welfare programmes will take care of the poor, leaving the rest of us, individually and corporately, to go our own sweet way. We must all respond by constructing pervasive and interwoven patterns in our lives – as persons, families, neighbours; as schools, as unions, as business enterprises, as churches – to live in such a way that there are no poor.

A business can not say it looks only after its shareholders and employees, while the government looks after the needy. The concern of a business is to produce in such a way that those in need, including employers and employees, neighbours and consumers, are able to live responsibly and healthily. A family must cherish its elderly and not abandon them to the sometimes not-so-tender ministrations of social workers and old age pensions. A union cannot look only to its members and pass by others in small, low-paying, uneconomic-to-organise sweatshops.

But, since our concern is with politics, we will concentrate on governmental responsibility. Government has a two-fold responsibility in respect to poverty:

(1) To develop an advisory, regulatory and legislative framework to ensure that societal institutions give people the resources to be free of poverty. It is to sanction and encourage businesses and unions to act in such a way that people have access to the goods necessary for them to live responsibly and creatively as image-bearers of God.

(2) When people are bound in poverty, government must, by its calling to justice, provide the means and opportunities for economic new birth. Those locked in poverty – the working poor, welfare mothers, the handicapped, the aged, the unemployed – must be given the opportunities of meaningful work to be able to support themselves and fulfil their life's responsibilities.

One aspect of our present society is that it tries to reverse the thrust of the Scriptures. We try to create prosperity and then hope we will have enough left over for the poor. We claim that the needs of the poor must be traded off against, or subordinated to, the growth of the economic system. *We live in such a way that the poor are forgotten* in the hope that if we do so then we will create prosperity so that, in the future, the poor can be taken care of. Another aspect of this faith is what is often called the 'trickle-down' theory – that if enough is produced, some of it will eventually trickle down to those who need it.

These two aspects are connected in the argument that 'you can't kill the goose that lays the golden eggs' – that we must produce more in order to create a surplus, in order to give tax revenue to the government which can then distribute the surplus to those in need. In short, the argument is that we must have the highest possible economic growth so that we can care for the poor.

Instead of this cycle of ignoring the poor to create a false abundance, a Christian understanding is that, as God's creatures, we must institute economic relations that do not *produce* poverty.

We need economic decisions that *in the first place* provide resources and new beginnings for those in need. Just as the Israelites had to trust God and pass two years without planting crops in the forty-ninth and fiftieth years, so we too must act with the economic trust that if we are faithful to the economic priorities that God wants then blessing will follow. We should not make a *goal* of prosperity and say that *then* we will take care of the poor. Rather we must take up the *way* of caring first for the poor, the widow, the fatherless and the sojourner, and rely on God's promise that those who do this will receive blessing (cf. Deut. 11). Our GNP indicators might not go up, but there will be peace and enough in the land.

Poverty and Stewardship

When we consider the biblical teaching concerning the poor and concerning stewardship, they point to the same conclusion – that from the very beginning we must act economically to bring life to the poor, to care for all God's creatures. When we weigh the benefits and costs of economic decisions we must look to the welfare of the poor as the benchmark of costs and benefits. These considerations will not lead us to a magic plan to abolish poverty for, in this sinful world, there will, as Jesus said, always be those who are poor. Nor will they directly lead us to a set of government policies. What they do lead us to is a commitment to act *first* for the poor.

In our society most of the poor are the unemployed, the aged (especially women), single parents (largely women) and their children, and those with low-paying jobs. In terms of a stewardly weighing of costs and benefits, unemployment must be seen as a vast cost. Despair, loneliness, illness and crime are all real economic costs. When we put the real weight of unemployment into our economic scales then most other considerations are counterbalanced. It is these needs that must be addressed first. No 'economic' policy can be successful if it does not address the poor first. No long-term social wellbeing, no real wealth, can come from a nation that is unrighteous in this. We must have stewardly economic decisions whose first question is costs and benefits to the poor.

CONCLUSIONS

The present responses to the problems of the welfare state do not get to the roots of our problems. The Tory strategy suggests building up more unpaid-for costs, which government will have

to pay for again, or which will work themselves out in the depriva-
tion and suffering of people, families, communities and the
environment. The conservatives must be challeged with their own
slogan, that 'there is no such thing as a free lunch'. We have to
pay for what we use; we have to deal with the real costs and
benefits to the poor. To opt for the *status quo* or to increase the
welfare state does not help us either. Such a policy is a refusal to
see that there *is* a real crisis of costs. While there is a concern for
the poor in this position it still does not face up to the fundamental
dis-location of economics in modern society.

Rather than debating how much or how little governments can
or should spend, we need to tackle our problems at their source.
We need to assess real costs and benefits, especially to the poor,
in our use of time, energy, resources, capital, fulfilling work, and
community life and *on that basis* decide whether or not to proceed
with an economic project. This is a task for companies, and also
for churches, communities, families and individuals. In the nature
of the case governments cannot force someone to be stewardly
(although they can make it more rewarding for people to be so).
Consequently there must be an internal renewal and commitment
in each area of life. We should not assume that economic redirection is solely a matter for governments. Without a real change of
heart, we will produce hollow legal frameworks and restrictions
which will, in their turn, produce other problems. So economics
points out the need for evangelism, including economic evangelism. Christians at work, in unions, in buying and selling, in using
things, must begin to move in the direction of stewardship.

There are also Christian economists around. A crucial task for
them is a redefinition of the basic economic categories that we use
in making decisions. 'Profits' must be re-understood as 'profitable'
things, as net benefits to healthy human life. 'Accounting' must
become the art of 'giving account' of what we have done with
what the Lord has given, just as we must give an account at the
last day. By redefining these categories we could start to analyse
what makes for stewardship and begin to plan stewardly political
policies. This is an integrally Christian question which, at the same
time, will require all of our present economic expertise to tackle.[13]
As Christian economists are unlikely to obtain funding for such a
project from present governments, corporations or foundations,
and as they are unlikely to find that such research results in a high
ranking from their professional colleagues, they will need all the
support, and all the types of support, that the church can give
them.

The government's mandate to do justice requires that it prevent
the economic oppression that unstewardly actions invariably

produce. Yet, at the same time, because governments are given only a specific task, we must beware of policies that would result in a virtual government take-over of economic life (see Chapter 3E). I would suggest three directions that governments could follow which might respect both these concerns:

(1) As corporations are unlikely to respond to a wide range of stewardly concerns unless they are held accountable for doing so, they should be restructured so as to allow worker, union, consumer and community voting representatives on the board of directors in numbers that together outweigh the voting power of the present shareholder representatives. This could become a legal requirement for larger corporations.

(2) The tax structure should reflect the amount of costs and benefits that company activities produce outside of themselves, rather than just reflecting the internal company accounts. Stewardly behaviour should be rewarded and unstewardly behaviour penalised. This could provide incentives for stewardship and could lead to efficiency, proficiency and the use of entrepreneurial skills in promoting stewardship.

(3) The government's own economic activities must place monetary, fiscal, economic and social policies within an overall framework of stewardship. Items such as money spent on job creation and job retraining should not be regarded as losses but as *investments*, which is what they are. The consumption of raw materials such as oil or land must not be treated merely as factors in producing income but as a loss of some of the real capital goods of the country, which they are. We must give account of losses in the natural, as well as the social, world so that we do not hold it cheaply.

These policies will be difficult to achieve, and, even then, they are tentative steps on the way. But they could at least set us off in the right direction and a step in the right direction is worth much more than many miles in the wrong direction. Nor are these policies ones which are guaranteed to produce wealth in the sense of an increase in the GNP. But real stewardship is, in its very nature, the preservation and creation of wealth in the sense of healthy human and natural life. If our destination is to have 'enough', then we must follow the path of stewardship.

6: International Relations and Nuclear Arms

NATIONALISM

When we deal with politics we deal with particular states, usually our own. We have the God given right and duty of citizens to be actively responsible for the affairs of our own country (see chapter 3F). It is this country's affairs that most affect us and our neighbours. Our governments are given the task to protect us from evildoers, including other governments and countries. Therefore we should not lose ourselves in internationalism as if we were citizens of the world only. We should not be ashamed to have a prior interest in and focus on the affairs of our own country. We should also be true patriots, having a love for our land and its ways. If we cannot love our own then we are seldom capable of loving anything else.

All of this is certainly true. But the realisation that we are members of a universal and transnational body, the body of Christ, means that we must challenge all forms of nationalism and chauvinism in our politics. We must have no part in the view that it is the purpose of government to aggrandise our country, or to see itself as the embodiment of a particular national will or genius. A state is an area which is united by a legal system into a political community that is responsible for administering public justice in that area. Countries can have, and usually do have, a variety of cultures, languages, religions and races within their boundaries. The state is not the embodiment of a culture, it is merely an agent for justice. Governments are not the 'leaders of the nation', they are simply the ones in charge of an area's political affairs.

While we have particular responsibilities for the affairs of the United Kingdom, we do not, first of all, act politically as 'British', but as Christians, followers of our great king, ones called to do the will of God in politics. Our aim is not to aggrandise our country or to see it win out over others, but to see that our governments do justly with a minimum of fuss.

Our membership in the worldwide body of Christ has immediate practical implications. For example, rather than drawing our information and judgments about other countries solely from the government or from British journalists, we should seek the witness and advice of our Christian kindred in other lands. We are 'neither Jew nor Greek' (Gal. 3:28). 'He is our peace, who has made us both one, and has broken down the dividing wall of hostility.' (Eph. 2:14) We must put flesh on the skeleton of our transnational body. We must meet with other Christians not only to learn of their churches and missions but to learn how they see their own politics and view our country. In the same way we must share with them what we see and think and do. How many of us know the words of the Nobel Peace Prize winner, fervent Christian, poet, Argentinian opposition activist, Perez Esquival, on the conflict over the Falkland Islands (or, as he would say, the Malvinas)? Would we heed those words or are we content to identify the Argentinians with their generals and assume that our fellow Christians there know nothing at all? Or again, how many of us knew before the visit of Pope John Paul II to Nagasaki, or even after it, that that town was the centre of Christianity in Japan when the second atomic bomb obliterated it? Or, considering that 60% of the world's Christians live in the Third World, should we not discuss with them the realities of world trade and aid? Do we realise that the Russian Orthodox Church, or the Baptists, or the pentecostals are also Russians, or do we equate the Russians with communists or 'the Kremlin'? As believers we have the task of developing a transnational Christian political mind and heart. From out of that mind and heart we must in turn act and take responsibility for our own country.

THE STATE OF THE WORLD

States

One of the most obvious facts about the political world today is that it is largely made up of *states*. This is not such a trite statement as it might first appear. If we use the word 'state' precisely (which in this book I often have not) then we mean a politically discrete entity, an area of land over which one government (or a federal arrangement of governments) exercises control. These political orders are distinct from families and churches, something not always true in the past. A world composed of such political units is quite a recent development.

For a long time there was no 'world' political order. The difficulties of travel meant that empires such as China or Persia had little to do with one another and each comprised their own universe. In China this is still largely true. Similar conditions prevailed in Europe where, until the decline of feudalism, there really were no states and the only continuing 'international relation' was 'Christendom' itself, then embodied in the institution of the Church.

There are still areas of the world where there are no real 'states', at least in the Western sense. Iran is now more of an eschatological religion in political form than it is a state, which is one reason why it does not act as nearly all other states want it to act. The Islamic world generally is still struggling with whether it is a group of states or whether Islam itself constitutes an overarching political order rather like medieval Christendom. In Lebanon right now there isn't any state, there is no abiding, enforceable legal order. In China the status of law is tenuous so that the country still reflects the characteristics of a personally run empire. The Soviet empire in eastern Europe makes it impossible to treat the relations between countries such as Poland and Czechoslovakia as if they were independent political units. Countries within American economic control, such as El Salvador, cannot maintain an independent foreign policy.

World Relations

In these brief comments about the world, we have already seen some of the variety of forces operating in international affairs. States, empires, religions, and civil conflicts all exert their influence. Apart from these matters we also have to consider the widespread influence of economic relations. We have become used to the terminology of the 'first world' (the democratic capitalist countries), the 'second world' (the communist countries) and the 'third world' (all the rest). These differences are also described as East/West and North/South. This scheme of understanding the world focusses on different economic systems and degrees of wealth. As the confrontation between the first and second world (with its possibilities of nuclear annihilation) is the major threat to the continuation of human life and as the confrontation between north and south largely reflects the boundary between those who are hungry and those who are not, there is a great deal to be said for understanding the world in these terms. However we should not be mesmerised by the categories of East/West and North/South. Clearly the idea of the 'South', or 'third world' is a catch-all of radically different countries. How much do Venezuela, Zimbabwe, Iran and South Korea actually have in common?

Earlier I emphasised the importance of religion as the final determinant of human social patterns. Its importance is now becoming apparent as, with the retreat of European colonialism, more and more of the world's cultures, hitherto rendered politically impotent, reassert themselves. The clearest example of this is the 'Islamic belt' stretching from Morocco on the Atlantic through Indonesia on the Pacific Rim. Religions such as Islam which have shaped civilisations, including the most powerful ones in the world, for over thirteen hundred years do not just pack their bags and give up just because European powers have taken them over for a century. What is occurring in Iran has taken its own particular Shiite form but it is symptomatic of the ferment in the Islamic world in general. Iran is not led by some crazy Ayatollah with a band of Mullahs, it is a manifestation of the resurgent power of a world religion.

Along these lines, we should re-think our conception of the 'West'. At one level the 'West' is one civilisation that has been shaped by Christianity, although it is now post-Christian. This 'West', which in this sense includes both Latin America and Eastern Europe, shows continuing common features and differences from the rest of the world. Similarly we should *not* think of the rest of the world just in terms of the western ideas of 'modernisation', 'development', 'secularisation' or 'liberation'. The world will not take on the patterns of the 'West', either of the 'first world' or of the communist bloc. Certainly 'modernisations' will occur, but they will take a variety of different forms. As Alexander Solzhenitsyn has pointed out, there are many 'worlds'. In international relations we should not think in the western terms of a world united in following 'reason' and seeking 'progress' but rather we must try to find out how countries and civilisations which are radically different from one another in their view of the world can exist alongside one another in peace.

If we do not re-understand the world in this way, then we will continue to be surprised at what happens about us. One reason the Americans were shocked and puzzled by what happened in Iran was that their political analysts in the State Department and the CIA were, like Marxists, trained to think only in western patterns. Prior to the revolution, their reports stressed what westerners think of as important – that the Shah had control of the army, that the politically influential classes were doing well economically and that there was at least some increase in wealth all across Iranian society. Consequently even as religious ferment boiled around them they kept stressing that the Shah was safe.

The rise of the 'non-West' is further shown by the patterns of military conflicts since the Second World War. The two 'world wars' of the twentieth century were the climaxes of tension between nation states *within* western civilisation.[1] (Russia is also part of western civilisation. Marxism is very much a European product.) There are still tensions here, such as in Northern Ireland, the Falklands and around the 'Iron Curtain'. But since World War II the major active military confrontations *between* states have taken place on the boundaries, the edges, of civilisations, particularly in those areas where western presences left over from colonial expansion still linger on in non-western territories. The Korean War, the Israeli-Palestinian conflicts, the Vietnam War, the civil war in Cyprus, the withdrawal of Portugal from Guinea-Bissau, Angola and Mozambique, the hostage crisis in Iran, the Russian invasion of Afghanistan, Mugabe's takeover of power in Zimbabwe and apartheid in South Africa and Namibia are all manifestations of these boundaries. There are now also renewed conflicts between other cultures, as with Iran and Iraq (Shiite Islam versus Arab Socialism), Ethiopia and Somalia (traditional Christian and Islamic countries fighting over artificial borders left by colonialists), and Chad (Islamic north versus Christian and pagan south). We should notice also that capitalism and communism, the two key components of modern, secular, western civilisation, usually have been maintained in the non-western world only through imposition by force on the part of authoritarian, tyrannic or totalitarian regimes which repress the freedoms and culture of the indigenous populations.

This is now the world we live in. The confrontations of North/South and of capitalism/communism are very real, but they are only one part of world relations. We must understand this if we are to begin to act in a way that brings justice to world affairs.

MODELS FOR HOW COUNTRIES DO AND SHOULD RELATE

With the breakdown of Christendom as a uniting element in Europe and with the emergence of distinct states, the questions of international relations, of how states do and should relate to one another, emerged.[2] People quickly tried to supply answers. In the sixteenth century Machiavelli suggested war and diplomacy. In the seventeenth century Hugo Grotius suggested international law. From out of these beginnings have grown the modern plethora of embassies, trade agreements, treaties, boundaries, standing armies and international organisations. The older practices of war, imperialism, and domination meanwhile have continued unabated.

Varieties of ways of understanding how states do and should

relate have been suggested. Coming out of nineteenth century
Europe, because of the success at the end of the Napoleonic wars
of the Treaty of Vienna in maintaining some semblance of peace
in Europe for the rest of the century, has come the idea of a
'balance of power'. The balance of power idea is that states will
usually do something dirty to one another if they can get away
with it, and so the only way to maintain peace is to ensure that
states, and possible alliances of states, are roughly equal in military power so that none can with confidence turn on its neighbours. Also coming out of this balance of power idea is the modern
theory of nuclear deterrence – maintaining defensible nuclear
arms with which one can retaliate so that no country can hope to
benefit itself via a nuclear attack. Another offshoot of the balance
of power ideas is the theory of 'realism' in international relations.
'Realism' believes that human beings or, at least, politically
powerful human beings or states, are self-deceptive and selfish
and that these traits explain how states relate to one another.
States will seek to be autonomous, to achieve their own interests
and expand their sphere of influence as much as they can. Hence,
international relations are, and can only be, power struggles. In
the last analysis the important power in international relations is
military power, and so each state must maintain sufficient armed
force to assert its interests. States that do not do so will not survive
in the long run: they will disappear or fall under the control of
another.

From out of the international law tradition has come a more
'idealistic' view of international relations. This view stresses
binding treaties between states, international legal agencies (such
as the International Court of Justice in the Hague) to mediate
disputes (such as the 'Cod War' with Iceland), and international
political bodies such as the United Nations. While not being dewy-
eyed about the capacity of states for evil, these views hold that
there is more to international relations than a power struggle.
Countries have at least some minimal sense of justice and are
willing to maintain compromises with others on that basis. Nowa-
days some people try to maintain a form of 'idealism' even without
assuming a desire for justice, for there are forces in the world, such
as nuclear war or the North/South conflict, which can threaten
the interests of *all* nations. It is argued that, in order to avoid
catastrophe, states, out of sheer *self-interest*, must surrender some
of their power and adhere to binding agreements. Related to these
'idealistic' theories is the theory of 'functionalism'. Functionalists
advocate developing *interdependence*, especially economic interdependence, between states. Their ground for doing so is that
states which have extensive trade links, investments in one

another's countries, and a division of labour between them are unlikely to fight because they have so many mutual interests and so both sides inevitably would lose much in a conflict. Such 'functionalism' has provided one of the basic rationales and motives for the development of the Common Market.

Theories of 'imperialism', especially economic imperialism, are also widespread, enough so as to be almost the orthodoxy of the left. This view stems from Lenin and (with differences) from the turn of the century English economist, J. A. Hobson. Lenin's theory basically holds that the rich countries have made, maintained and kept their wealth because they have exploited and drawn wealth out of the countries which are now poor. Even though political empires have now largely gone, at least from the third world, this view maintains that 'economic empires', basically trade and investment links managed through multinational corporations, still continue a pattern of exploitation and that this explains most of the continuing poverty in the third world. Such a theory does not necessarily specify a picture of how states can relate for it has both a 'realist' and an 'idealist' version. The realist version (Lenin's) holds that the capitalist powers will maintain their exploitation as long as they can, and can only be stopped by armed struggle, as in Cuba, Nicaragua or El Salvador. On the other hand, socialist powers are assumed to be able to co-exist peacefully. The idealist version take a softer view of the predelictions of capitalist and socialist states and attempts to overcome the patterns of exploitation by means of international agreements and treaties, such as the recent proposal for a New International Economic Order.

There are other views of international relations besides these but most of them are really methods for exploring how nations behave. Furthermore the theories we have mentioned are not incompatible for, as we have seen, there can be both 'idealistic' and 'realistic' theories of imperialism. Functionalism can also fit either of the schemes, though it is stressed more by the idealists. Consequently we shall focus on the polarity of 'idealistic' and 'realistic' views of international relations.

This polarity is, of course, a rather simplistic way of looking at the matter, and the terms themselves are hardly adequate. Who, after all, wants to be called merely an 'idealist' and who does not want to be reckoned a 'realist'? Nevertheless this polarity does illuminate some of the major views about in international relations. It corresponds fairly well to the differences about the feasibility of restructuring world trade and aid and it illustrates some of the major differences about nuclear armament and disarmament.

Consequently we will use this polarity to suggest how we as Christians should approach relations between countries.

A CHRISTIAN APPROACH TO INTERNATIONAL RELATIONS

Idealism, Realism and Justice

There is something in both idealism and realism that should appeal to us as Christians. As far as realism is concerned we know that human beings are fallen, that a desire for power – to be like God – is at the root of the fall, and that human perfection is not to be expected in this world. Consequently we should not act in the world as though it were run on good will and amity. Indeed realist theory rests on a long tradition of Christian reflection about politics stretching back at least as far as Saint Augustine. Perhaps the most articulate twentieth-century exponent of such realism in the West was the great American theologian, Reinhold Niebuhr.

But we cannot let the matter rest with realism. Sin and hunger for power are not the only things to be said about action in God's world. God has not deserted the world, human beings are still called to do justice and they have not lost the image of God. Following the way of the Lord is still the route to blessing. As God's children we cannot avoid trying to create and maintain just relationships between nations. In this sense we have to be 'idealistic'. Idealism too, as manifested in such people as Hobson and former United States President Jimmy Carter, draws on a long Christian tradition.

Consequently, to be Christian in our international relations we must be both 'idealistic' and 'realistic'. The fact that governments are given the 'power of the sword', including the authority to coerce, shows that this is something that they actually need in this sinful world. A government which does not maintain its ability to defend its citizens is not only naive but is also shirking its God-given responsibility (which is perhaps only another way of saying the same thing).

But this ability to defend one's legitimate interests does not by itself give any guidance at all to what else governments *ought* to be doing in relation to others. Maintaining their ability to act does not tell them *how* else to act. In this sense realism cannot be a guide to international conduct, for it merely cautions states what to beware of. It gives them no direction as to *what* they should and can seek to achieve. Governments like everything else in God's creation, are given a task to do: they exist *for* particular reasons, to *do* particular things. Governments are not haphazard constructions of human beings which are free to take up or drop anything they find interesting or distasteful. They are ordained by God for the task of doing of justice – *including justice in international relations*. This is not a responsibility which can be shirked.

This responsibility to seek just international relations is not a mandate to construct an ideal order, as though there were a given, fixed state of affairs which is just and which, when achieved, would abolish the need for further action. Justice is not a mandate either to expect or to try to construct a utopia. It is not a *goal* to be achieved. It is, as we have tried to show, a *way* to be followed. Acting justly is the way we are to follow in the day to day affairs of international relations. Consequently, international justice is not something that could only exist in an ideal world of peace-loving states. It is something which is our guide right now, right here, in our broken world of despotic and self-seeking states. . Following justice is not unrealistic, as though it assumes that there is universal good will when this is clearly not the case. A search for justice must be intensely realistic about the world and seek to act justly in such a world. States cannot retreat into self-interest and mere realism because the world is wicked but, precisely because the world is wicked, they must harness their ability to act justly.

As this need to do justice is not merely some ideal existing in the clouds somewhere but is an aspect of the actual way God has made the world we live in, then its reality is manifested, however brokenly, in what states actually do even now. This is shown, for example, in balance of power relations. A balance of power, if it is to secure peace, needs to be much more than merely a military stand-off. For if one state feels unjustly suppressed then it will take pains to upset the balance and so there cannot be stability. A successful balance of power arrangement is one which the participants feel is *legitimate*, is one whose arrangements can be justified. The arrangement might not be their first choice for inter-state relations but they accept it as giving a relatively just place to themselves and their neighbours. Put in another way, there must be a concensus that the balance of power arrangement is relatively fair or just. Without such a concensus about international arrangements then every disagreement immediately becomes a test of strength and no negotiations are possible. Here we can see that a sense of justice is itself an essential component of international relations: it is itself *part of the reality*. Justice is not a pipedream but an essential aspect of politics itself. If we ignore justice in international relations then we ignore part of reality and we delude ourselves.

Sovereignty

Another aspect of the priority of justice is that we must turn away from the doctrine of 'national sovereignty'. Briefly put, such sovereignty asserts that, subject only to the constraints of its own population, a state can do what it likes and nobody else can legitimately stop it. Such a view not only challenges any overriding conception of justice but is also empirical nonsense, for it is quite clear that as soon as any two 'sovereign' states assert a claim to the same thing, they cannot both be legitimate. One state's 'sovereignty' will always run into another state's 'sovereignty' and they cannot both be supreme. In fact, logically, there can be only one sovereign in the world at one time.

Christians must resist claims to state, or national, 'sovereignty' on the simple grounds that *only God is sovereign*. This is not some piece of theological sleight-of-hand disguising two very different meanings of 'sovereign', for the sovereignty of God is always of immediate political relevance. Because God is sovereign there can be no 'sovereignty', no final authority, in anything on earth. All peoples, all governments, are always required to conform their actions to the authority that God has given not only to them but also to others, whether other countries or other institutions such as churches or families. In concert with their neighbours, states must subordinate their authority to the doing of justice. This awareness of the limits of sovereignty, coupled with our earlier remarks about the rule of law, should lead us to stress treaties and international law as a possible means of Christian response to international conflicts in the modern age.

The Need for Limits

We should couple the limits on sovereignty with the fact of idolatry. An idol is anything put in the place of God. Anything that is pursued *without limits* is, almost by definition, an idol. *If we set up a goal, whether that be state sovereignty, or military security, or national prosperity, and subordinate everything else to that goal then we have made our goal into an idol.* Therefore we should always consider the limits of what we seek. We must always ask 'under what circumstances will we give up or lessen our goal?'

What might cause us to limit our military security – would it be human rights, the wellbeing of other countries, the decrease of nuclear tensions? Is there anything for which we will lessen our security? If we cannot find an answer to this question or if our answer is no then it is clear that we are following an idol. If we can find an answer to these questions, then we must ask whether these conditions for relinquishing or lessening our goals already exist. In many cases we will find that they do. Hence, following God rather than following an idol would require us to decrease our security or relinquish our wealth. Failure to do so would be idolatry, it would be a violation of the first and second of the ten commandments. In the light of our need for limits, we will now consider one key problem of modern politics – the nuclear arms race. We will begin by considering Christian views of war and the limits of war.

CHRISTIAN VIEWS OF WAR

Pacifism and 'Just-War' Views

The question of warfare has been a central and divisive element of Christian views of politics since the beginning of the Christian Church. Christians have taken a variety of views including launching crusades or simply going along with whatever a government asks. Nevertheless there are really only two longstanding, official and worked-out Christian approaches to warfare. These are the pacifist and the just war traditions.

The pacifist or non-violent tradition holds that Christians cannot engage in warfare or violence. There are a range of disagreements within this broad framework. These include whether police functions should be rejected in the same way as military functions, or whether Christians can serve in non-combatant roles, such as medical officers or air raid wardens, or whether only Christians or the government itself must forsake violence.

The key text for the Christian pacifist view is, obviously, the Sermon on the Mount – 'blessed are the meek', 'turn the other cheek', 'love your enemies and pray for those who persecute you' and so forth (Matt. 5). Coupled with this are other texts such as 'all who take the sword will perish by the sword' (Matt. 26:52). The pacifist asks how, faced with such clear and unequivocal injunctions, any Christian could justify doing violence to anybody, including our enemies.

Of course, there are other parts of the Scripture which seem to speak differently. God urges Israel to (certain) wars in the Old Testament and these are called 'wars of the Lord' (cf. Num. 21:14, Josh. 3:5). The pacifist response to these is that Jesus is clearly the culmination and fullness of God's revelation to us and that God's will becomes only gradually apparent in the Old Testament so that what Jesus says and lives must supercede all that has gone before. There are also New Testament texts such as 'he who is in authority . . . is God's servant for your good . . . he does not bear the sword in vain' (Romans 13:3, 4). The Christian pacifist response to this is to accept the teaching but to say that, in the light of Jesus' words and life, the state cannot then be part of the gospel, the new order of *redemption* in Jesus Christ. The state is then seen as part of God's *preserving* grace whereby sin is restrained. Christians may be thankful for what the state does but, as ones committed to the new order of Jesus Christ, we should obey what he has said and not participate in the fallen order of the state.

As will be clear from the earlier discussions in this book, I do not agree with the pacifist position. The distinction between 'God's order of preservation' (outside of Jesus Christ) and 'God's order of redemption' (in Jesus Christ) does not appear to me to hold water. The authority of the state is, like *all* genuine authority, in Jesus Christ. The distinction between Matthew five and Romans thirteen is not one between a 'Christian order' and a 'preservation order': rather, it is a distinction between ordinary persons and those with the authority of government office (as, I think, the juxtaposition of Rom. 12:9 and 13:4 shows).

The key just-war texts are Romans thirteen and 1 Peter 2:13–17, which state that governments are God's appointed servants and that essential to their task in this sinful world is the 'power of the sword.' These texts indicate that the use of force, while terrible and to be avoided, is something that God authorises for our governments, at least in a fallen situation. While no Christian person should hate their enemy or do violence to their neighbour, even in retaliation, this is distinct from a Christian, or anybody else, in the God-given *judicial* function of deterring and paying back evildoers. Just war theorists also tend to see much more agreement between the Old and the New Testaments pointing out that the root of the Old Covenant is just as much love and grace as is the New, and that right after the Beatitudes Jesus goes on to say 'Think not that I have come to abolish the law and the prophets . . .' (Matt. 5:17).

Given that the use of force by governments is something authorised by God, just war theorists look for biblical guidance for that use and, as the New Testament does not involve wars, then the Old Testament is looked to for such guidance. In the wars of Israel we find the following limits on warmaking:
(a) With certain restrictions all those over twenty could be 'called-up' (Num. 1:2, 3) but usually only selected people were (Num. 31:3–6).
(b) Certain people were exempted from the 'call-up' (Deut. 20:1–8), including

i) those who had built a new house but had not dedicated it or enjoyed it.

ii) those who had planted a vineyard and not enjoyed its fruit.

iii) those who had 'betrothed a wife and not taken her' (as they would have a divided mind). This is beautifully depicted in Deuteronomy 24:5 'When a man taketh a new wife, he shall not go out in the host, neither shall he be charged with any business; he shall be free at home one year, and shall cheer up his wife' (King James Version).

iv) 'the fearful and faint hearted'.

v) the Levites.

Here we see that marriage, housing and farming were not taken up into a total war effort. These activities have their own place in God's world and must be respected. The needs of the state cannot override the needs of others.

(c) Israel had to declare war or offer peace before any attack (Deut. 23:9–14).

(d) Captured women could not be made slaves or kept as permanent captives, but could be married (Deut. 2:10–14).

(e) The war must be *defensive*. Israel was forbidden to use more than a limited number of horses (Deut. 17:16), and therefore chariots, because horses and chariots were weapons used in *offence*.

(f) Israel was not to cut down fruit trees even for a seige. They could only use non-fruit trees and only as much as they needed for 'are the trees in the field men, that they should be beseiged by thee?' The war could not be against the earth, even against the enemies' earth (Deut. 20:19, 20).

From a consideration of these types of examples the idea of a 'just war' has developed – an acceptance within strong limits of governmental use of force against aggressors. Traditionally, in this view, these texts have been interpreted so as to give the following basic criteria of a just war:

(a) That the intention of the war is good. Its goal must not be gain but a just peace.

(b) The cause must be justified. It must be a defence against aggression – usually meaning the defence of one's own territory.

(c) The means must be limited. This implies that:

i) Non-combatants, neutrals and third parties cannot be harmed.

ii) Existing laws and treaties, e.g. the Geneva Convention on the rules of war, must be honoured.

iii) The means must be proportionate to the goals. The war must not do more harm than good: you don't kill a thousand to save a hundred.

iv) The enemy must know the terms on which peace can be achieved.

v) The goal must be the return of the aggressor to a rightful place among the nations – not its extermination or subjugation.

(d) The war must be winnable: ie. one should not engage in futile warfare but only to achieve a realisable goal.

(e) The war must be a matter of last resort. All other means must have been tried.

(f) Only a duly constituted government can wage such a war. Private citizens cannot do so.

One should note that this is not a 'shopping list' of unrelated items, but that it has an intrinsic logic. The logic is that our neighbours, even our enemies, have a right not to be harmed, indeed that they must must be loved. So, if we do harm them, then it must be only with a powerful justification. We must always ask 'in whose name, for what cause, with what intention, within what limits?'

There are a variety of divisions within just war theory, notably whether, if waging an unjust war, the government should be opposed or only tolerated and whether a just war should meet all of the criteria outlined or only a substantial part of them.

History of Views of War

It is often argued that for its first three and a half centuries, the Christian Church was pacifist in outlook. But there is not a great deal of evidence on this matter either way, and what evidence there is is often ambiguous. What is clear is that it was only in the fourth century, with the first official 'Christian' Roman Emperor, Constantine, that just war views became dominant. This association between just war views and the political accomodation of Christianity with the Empire should make us suspicious as to whether the Church was selling its soul in accepting this view of war. Indeed, many pacifists, and many Christians who are not pacifists, take the view that the official acceptance of Christianity by the Roman Empire signalled a turning away from the purity and simplicity of the early Church, a purity and simplicity to which we must return.

But we should beware of exaggerating the purity of the early Church. The goings on at Corinth, for example, were a level of corruption to match anything in later history (1 Cor. 5–11). Nor, in view of the fact that the Christian Church is meant to develop historically, should we think that new things in the Church are necessarily wrong things. In the time of Constantine, whatever the merits of the supposed 'Christianisation' of the Empire, Christians, hitherto suppressed and persecuted, were faced with the actual responsibility of *holding* political power. A pacifist view may be cogent among people who could not affect political events anyway but start to appear to be quite wrong when those same people had to decide about the actual use of government power. Just war theories can also be understood not necessarily as a compromise with imperial power but as a consistent elaboration of the Church's teaching as it faced new situations and responsibilities. Since that time just war views have become almost the orthodoxy in the Church and have become the dominant view among Christians in the twentieth century.

Meanwhile the Christian pacifist tradition has persisted. A pacifist witness was upheld by the early Franciscans and came to an important expression in the Reformation amongst the Anabaptists. It has continued until the present in the historic 'peace churches' such as the Mennonites. With the threat of nuclear destruction over our heads these 'peace churches' are taking their mission seriously and Christian pacifist views have become much more widespread amongst Christians, especially younger ones, in nearly all Christian traditions.

It must be stressed that just-war views were *not* intended as *justifications* for war. They were not, in principle, to show how Christians could go to war. Rather, they were developed as means of *preventing* war, as guarding against it. They operated against the background of the assumption that war was a terrible thing and that it was to be avoided at almost any cost. They were *limits* placed on warmaking, stringent conditions that had to be met in any consideration of war.

Peacemaking

Christian pacifism and just war theories were essentially negative, they were intended to stop war. The positive Christian teaching in this matter was to *pursue peace*. The entire Scriptures point us to the vocation of peacemaking. It is true that the peace of Scripture, *shalom*, is far more than an uneasy international truce. *Shalom* also has the meaning of universal health, prosperity and peace with God. But this peace certainly includes the absence of armed conflict. It is also true that there will be no final peace until the return of the Messiah. But, nevertheless, we are commanded to work for peace, just as we are commanded to follow all areas of God's will although none will reach its final reflection. Isaiah looks forward to the day when 'they shall beat their swords into plowshares' (Isa. 2:4), a vision which is now inscribed on the United Nations building in New York. The Psalmist rejoices that 'justice and peace will kiss one another' (Ps. 85:10). Jesus blesses the peacemakers and he is himself the Prince of Peace (Isa. 9:6. See also Luke 1:79; 2:14). The Christian aim is not to allow for war but to do those things that make for peace.

Lack of Christian Integrity

One final comment may be made about the just war tradition. Tragically, it has usually had little effect on the peacemaking practice of Christians. We have usually gone along with our governments and accepted their propaganda no matter what. We have generally been like the British and German Christians in the first World War, who each proclaimed 'God is on our side'. But the fact that we have ignored the provisions of just war theory does not invalidate them, any more than the fact that most people have never been persuaded to be pacifists invalidates that tradition, or any more than the fact that our violating other commandments invalidates them. There are also particular achievements of just war theory that must be recognised, such as the development of international law and of military codes of conduct like the Geneva Convention.

But we must take Christian teaching on these matters much more seriously than we have in the past. If we take our obedience to God seriously then we should not be subservient to our governments. We must soberly consider the example of Jeremiah who refused to support the people of Judah in their wars with Babylon because they were unjust. He prophesied that 'the whole land shall be a desolation' (Jer. 4:27), that 'a nation from afar . . . shall eat up your sons and daughters' (5:15, 16) and he was cursed by all (4:27; 5:15, 16; 15:10). He was imprisoned by Zedekiah King of Judah, for prophesying that the city would fall even as the Babylonians were beseiging Jerusalem (32:1–5; 33). He was accused of being a deserter and traitor and was beaten, imprisoned, starved and threatened with death (26:11; 37:11–15; 38:1–6; 43:1–3). Jeremiah did not 'rally round the flag', to put it mildly. He denounced what Judah did even at its time of greatest crisis and he faced death for doing so. Just war doctrines could demand similar things of us in our day.

NUCLEAR WAR AND DETERRENCE

A 'No' to Waging Nuclear War

On Christian pacifist grounds it is clearly evil to start or to wage a nuclear war. Just war views lead to the same conclusions because it is impossible for any nuclear exchange to meet the just war criteria we have outlined. No war which would scorch the earth and annihilate humankind, or leave alive only a wretched fragment of it, can possibly respect the lives of the innocent, honour existing laws of war, achieve peace with the enemy or return an aggressor to its rightful place among the nations. Both sets of consistent Christian teaching point to the same conclusion – no government that seeks to be obedient to God can wage nuclear war.

Let me re-emphasise that this is not a pacifist position. It is simply the outcome of the realisation that any legitimate force in God's world must be limited. John Howard Yoder is right to point out that, with respect to nuclear war, the essential difference is not between pacifists and just war theorists, it is between those that take historical Christian teaching, of whatever stripe, seriously and those who do not.[3] Further, as just war theories are given confessional status in the Lutheran churches' *Augsburg Confession*, the Presbyterians' and Congregationalists' *Westminster Confession* and the Anglicans' *Thirty Nine Articles*, then any member of these churches who would wage such a war is in violation of these confessions and should be considered a candidate for church discipline. In this way churches, without becoming political bodies but simply by upholding sound doctrinal standards, can contribute to the cause of peacemaking. This also illustrates the point that Christian politics not only calls for Christian evangelism, and vice versa, but for good church order as well.

It may be responded that a refusal to engage in nuclear war may be clearly Christian but that such a position is not really relevant to our present disputes. After all – there is nobody who is in *favour* of nuclear war! But a refusal to engage in nuclear conflict does have some bite. It asserts that nuclear conflict cannot be used to achieve political goals, and this at least cuts out certain Pentagon Generals and Soviet Marshalls. Further, a refusal of nuclear war means that one cannot plan to win such a war – and this contradicts much of current United States nuclear policy under Reagan. As we shall see later, it also requires us to oppose certain overall trends in western, and of course eastern, nuclear planning. The realisation that we must avoid nuclear war means that it is impossible for any Christian to accept a 'first-strike' nuclear policy. A 'first-strike' policy holds that, in response to an attack with 'conventional' (ie. non-nuclear) arms, we would be prepared to retaliate with a nuclear attack, we would be prepared to *start* a nuclear war. This is the present policy of NATO and it is one which we should not support. It is a policy which must be abandoned.

But the avoidance of nuclear war does not itself answer many of our basic questions about nuclear armament and disarmament. The chief justification of nuclear armament and rearmament is, after all, that it is a *deterrent*, that it is a way of *stopping* your enemies from attacking, that it is a means, perhaps the only means, of actually *preventing* nuclear war.

Deterrence

Although its ramifications are complex, the basic idea of deterrence is quite simple.[4] If each side has at its disposal enough nuclear weapons with which it could retaliate then nobody would be insane enough to attack in the first place for it would result in the effective destruction of both sides. Such deterrence is the *official* nuclear stance of the Warsaw Pact countries and, except for its 'first strike' position, of NATO. Each side claims that its nuclear arms have only one purpose, that of *deterring* a possible or actual enemy. But, as we shall see in the next section, since many nuclear policies in the 1980's do *not* appear to be based on deterrence, then we must be very clear about what deterrence is and, more particularly, what it is not.

(a) Deterrence is only deterrence *against nuclear attack*. It cannot be used as a deterrent against a conventional attack, such as an invasion of Western Europe by the Soviet Union. The threat to use *nuclear* weapons against a *conventional* attack is a threat to *start* a nuclear conflict and, therefore, is no longer solely a deterrent *to* nuclear attack.

(b) Because of the limitation of nuclear deterrence to *deterring a nuclear attack*, then nuclear weapons cannot be an instrument of foreign policy. One cannot threaten another nation with nuclear attack to make it 'behave' properly, for this would be a threat to start a nuclear war. This means that, as long as we want deterrence to hold, nuclear force will be irrelevant to world conflicts. This is in fact largely the case now. The Soviets cannot impose their will on Afghanistan through nuclear weapons, nor can the United States force the Soviet Union to leave Afghanistan through nuclear weapons. Nuclear arms are irrelevant to the Falklands, to the hostage crisis in Iran, to the revolution in Nicaragua or the civil war in El Salvador. Indeed, as the former United States Ambassador to the Soviet Union, George F. Kennan, pointed out over thirty years ago, any country which relies on nuclear weapons as the basis of its military strength and foreign policy is liable to find itself helpless and impotent in all areas, except that it will not be attacked by nuclear arms.[5]

(c) Nuclear deterrence has nothing to do with *winning* a nuclear war or achieving *superiority* over an enemy. It is a means of *preventing* such a war, not winning or being successful once a war has started.

(d) Deterrence has nothing to do with having *more* nuclear weapons than, or an *equal* number of nuclear weapons as an enemy. Deterrence means having sufficient nuclear weapons to have the potential to inflict unacceptable damage on an enemy even if the enemy has launched a nuclear attack. The number of nuclear weapons an enemy has is *per se* irrelevant.

(e) Deterrence must be a *mutual* thing. To avoid nuclear war *both* sides (or *all* sides) must believe that they can deter an enemy from a nuclear attack. It is as important to deterrence theory that the enemy is as secure from attack as we are ourselves. If one side builds up its forces so that an enemy feels that its own nuclear deterrent could be wiped out without a chance of retaliation in the event of a pre-emptive attack, then deterrence no longer works. If one side is made to feel vulnerable then the chances of its launching a nuclear attack are increased. Hence deterrence requires *not having too many* nuclear weapons, *not* having weapons of the *wrong type* (i.e. those capable of destroying the enemy's deterrent), and *not threatening* one's enemy. *Each side must preserve the safety of the other*. For deterrence to work there must be cooperation, either extrinsic or intrinsic, between the two sides.

This is, broadly, what nuclear deterrence is and is not. Seen in this light it is clear that many of our current nuclear actions have very little to do with deterrence. The repeated stress on whether the Russians have more or fewer nuclear weapons than we do is irrelevant to deterrence unless it is shown that such weapons threaten our deterrent forces. A 'first strike' policy is a contradiction of deterrence. Planning to win a nuclear war or threatening an enemy is a violation of deterrence.

A Conditional Acceptance of Deterrence

How should we evaluate deterrence as a Christian means of preventing nuclear war? Obviously, what we want to achieve is the eradication of nuclear weapons. But how are we to go about achieving that, and what do we do in the meantime? Is deterrence acceptable as a step on the road to nuclear disarmament? Deterrence is a very dangerous way to live, but there do not appear to be other acceptable alternatives. The policy of unilateral disarmament, of one side dismantling all its nuclear weapons, does not appear to make nuclear war less likely. Apart from leaving one open to nuclear blackmail, it could invite nuclear attack from an unscrupulous enemy. If we are concerned to prevent nuclear war then there is little reason to suppose that unilateral disarmament would help us do so. Multilateral nuclear disarmament appears to offer the most substantial hope but we should note that even here there are problems. It seems extremely unlikely that we will forget how to build such weapons and so the possibility of one side rearming and threatening war will always remain. Not only nuclear weapons themselves but the *mere possibility of being able to build them* has changed the structure of international relations. Total multilateral disarmament can only offer security against nuclear war if it is accompanied by the most rigorous safeguards and inspection systems to prevent someone from rebuilding, and, even then, the risk will not totally be gone.

If these are the options then I think that we must push our governments to strive for total multilateral disarmament with rigorous inspection of compliance. While striving for this end we can accept nuclear deterrence as a means of preventing nuclear war. Therefore, I believe that Christians should, at this time, support a policy of nuclear deterrence as I have outlined it.[6]

Accepting such deterrence does not mean accepting the *status quo*. It means maintaining only sufficient nuclear arms to deter an enemy from attacking. Presently one Polaris submarine (which may be replaced by the larger Trident) *by itself* possesses enough force to severely damage the Soviet Union. Hence, we have no need for the vast array of tens of thousands of nuclear weapons possessed by NATO. If we are serious about deterring the Soviet Union, rather than threatening it, then we could immediately and unilaterally dismantle about half of our nuclear weapons. This would still leave more than adequate deterrence. The Soviet Union may follow this example, which would move us closer to genuine multilateral disarmament, but whether it does or does not is irrelevant to deterrence.

Deterrence means making sure that the nuclear weapons we now possess are safe from destruction in a nuclear attack upon them. The only possible justification for installing new weapons is that they are safer from attack than previous ones. This is the argument that President Reagan is using to justify replacing the older United States 'Minutemen' missiles with the newer 'MX'. But in this case the argument is tenuous. The United States has more than enough deterrent capability in its bomber fleets and its almost invulnerable submarine fleets.

Deterrence also means that we must *not threaten the Soviet Union*. In particular, we must not install any nuclear weapons which could threaten the Soviets' own nuclear weapons and, hence, its ability to retaliate against us. Let us be quite clear that deterrence means that we must take pains to safeguard the Soviet Union from nuclear attack and that we must not threaten its survival.

As we have noted, deterrence also means that NATO must abandon its position that it will use 'battlefield' *nuclear* weapons to retaliate against a Warsaw Pact invasion of Western Europe using *conventional* weapons. No responsible observer believes that such a nuclear retaliation could end up in anything but full scale nuclear war.[7] NATO must accept a 'no first use of nuclear weapons' policy.[8] If we believe that the Warsaw Pact countries are liable to invade Western Europe then we must defend ourselves with conventional means and, if necessary, build up our conventional forces to be able to do so.

Finally, deterrence means serious negotiation and agreement with the Soviet Union. We are often told that negotiation with the Soviet Union is next to useless because the Russians do not bargain in good faith. People who stress disarmament are criticised as naive simpletons who simply do not understand the reality of the Soviet menace. These criticisms are irrelevant to what we have said here. Such negotiations and disarmament do not imply that the Russians (or the Americans or anybody else) are really quite generous and peace loving. It only implies that we and the Russians have a common interest in not being dead. On the basis of this common interest we can find agreement. Even those who see Soviet policy as bent on achieving world domination must give the Russians credit for understanding that such world domination would be greatly hindered if Soviet cities were reduced to glassy, black slag that glows in the dark.

THE PRESENT NUCLEAR BUILD UP

Current Arms Proposals

Currently the chief item of nuclear contention is the installation since the fall of 1983 of 108 Pershing II and 463 cruise missiles in western Europe. In Britain this is coupled with the proposed purchase of D-5 Trident submarine launched missiles from the United States. The justification offered for these new weapons is that since 1976 the Soviet Union has replaced its older missiles in Europe with 243 of the more accurate, faster, longer range SS-20's. In 1978 President Carter proposed that the USSR should stop its introduction of these new intermediate-range missiles and, in return, NATO would then not modernise its own European forces by introducing the intermediate range Pershing II and cruise missiles. The USSR refused to do so and currently has several hundred SS-20s in place. President Reagan later offered the 'zero-zero' option – that if the Soviets take all their missiles out, then NATO will not introduce any of its own. The Soviet Union has, in turn, offered to reduce its number of missiles to 162, which is equivalent to the number of intermediate range missiles held by Great Britain and France. NATO's stance has been, although it is now shifting, that their nuclear weapons are not part of the NATO forces and should not be counted in the totals.

What does our previous discussion of deterrence indicate about this controversy? The rationale usually offered for the introduction of these new weapons is couched in the form of deterrence theory. It is said that the Pershing and the cruise missile will create an intra-European stand-off, which would be a legitimate application of deterrence. The further rationale for this proposed intra-European deterrence, as distinguished from deterrence between the United States and the Soviet Union, is basically that if the Soviet Union launched a nuclear attack on western Europe *only* then Europeans have no guarantee that the United States would retaliate against the USSR. In short, the rationale is the fear that the United States would rather 'lose' Europe than join in the nuclear conflict and, inevitably, be wiped out itself. In this view American nuclear weapons would *not* deter a nuclear attack on Europe. Hence the need for Europe's own Pershing II's and cruise missiles.

From what we have said so far about deterrence, this might at first appear quite acceptable as an example of deterrence. However, if we consider the nature of these new weapons and the dynamics of the arms race then it appears doubtful that these weapons will in fact help deterrence. First we will consider the dynamics of the arms race.

The Escalation of Warfare

At present the number, type, strength and accuracy of nuclear weapons is increasing. Hundreds of billions of dollars have been diverted from healthier uses in order to maintain these weapons. The arms race itself is like a spiral. Each side takes a benign view of its own weapons and the uses to which they *will* be put, and takes a suspicious view of the other's weapons and the uses to which they *can* be put. Hence there is always an imbalance in how the sides see their own situation. Each feels vulnerable and claims that it has no option but to respond to the possible threat of the other and so the build-up goes inexorably on. Each attempt at arms control (with the exception of the ABM treaty) has only accepted what has been done already in the past and has only provided a basis for further types of increase. We are all conscious that this spiral has led us absolutely nowhere in terms of security. We are at least as vulnerable, and probably more so, than we were twenty years ago. This process of an obsession with security producing ever less security has the hallmarks of what we earlier called idolatry. The history of this idolatry can be traced back beyond the beginning of the nuclear age.

The nuclear arms race appears to be a continuation, at a more lethal level, of a dynamic which has been shaping warfare for at least the last two centuries. We live in the century of *total war*, a century in which it has become an accepted fact that tens of millions or hundreds of millions of people may be exterminated by governments as they pursue their goals. Of course there have been total wars before. There has never been a 'golden age' when war was always fought within accepted limits. Attila the Hun, for example, was not an exponent of just-war theories. But in the past our countries have in principle if not in practice, rejected the idea of war without limits.

At one time war was ostensibly for professionals: the average citizen was not assumed to have to fight. But after the French Revolution France required all citizens to fight, and Napoleon continued this practice with, for a while, much success. This total mobilisation was criticised by Napoleon's opponents but, gradually, they too accepted this practice. At one time we distinguished between attacking soldiers and attacking civilians. We were horrified that the Germans bombed allied cities in World War One. But this practice became accepted too and it bore its evil fruit in the Spanish Civil War and World War Two when attacks, by all sides, killed thousands of civilians and became common practice. London was attacked, and in return Berlin was attacked tenfold. The inhabitants of Dresden were roasted with fire-bombing. Hiroshima and its people were removed from the face of the earth.

In all of these cases the attackers maintained that the attack was actually on military and strategic targets but that it was impossible to get those targets without hitting civilians. In this way the distinction has become an academic one and, in the case of a nuclear attack, it is invidious double talk. An attack which we *know* will kill tens of millions of children, not to mention anybody else, cannot be regarded by any stretch of the imagination as safeguarding innocent life.

It is not just that these things were done. Something like them nearly always has been, although at a technically less proficient, and therefore less destructive, level. It is also that these practices are now being accepted with few, and eventually no, qualms. We have begun to accept them as legitimate actions. In the nuclear age we contemplate total war against all enemy resources, including civilians, including children, including nature. Like some misbegotten Samsons we threaten to pull the earth down about us.

Hence, we must consider present strategies not only in the light of deterrence theory and avoiding nuclear war, but also in the light of the development of modern warfare. We are refusing to recognise any limits on our power to defend ourselves. Our quest for security, quite legitimate in itself, has become an absolute goal, an idol, so that we will not allow anything to happen which might lessen our security. If mobilising the whole society seems to increase our security, we will do it. If destroying civilians seems to increase our security then we will do it. If threatening to destroy the earth seems to increase our security (a strange thing) then we will do it. No limits to our security will be tolerated. Traditional Christian teaching on war is often dismissed in the nuclear age as 'naive' and 'idealistic', if not even as sympathy for the USSR. This is an idolisation of security and its effect is to decrease any real security.

The Problems of New Weapons

Several new developments by both NATO and the Warsaw Pact make nuclear war more likely. Some of these new weapons systems and their effects are:

(a) The development of the neutron bomb (a bomb with a relatively small blast but lots of radiation) is supposed to further the development of 'battlefield nuclear weapons' because it could destroy the crews of Russian tanks invading western Europe while leaving the towns and cities still standing. But such a weapon lowers the 'threshold' of nuclear warfare, it envisages new situations short of a Soviet nuclear attack in which NATO would *start* using nuclear weapons. It makes nuclear war easier to begin. Consequently it increases the nuclear danger to us all.

(b) The cruise missile flies beneath the level of radar detection and therefore is harder to detect. This, coupled with the greater speed and precision of other new missiles, cuts down the 'response time' to a possible nuclear attack from about twenty minutes to six minutes, perhaps less in western Europe. 'Response time' is the amount of time between when someone discovers they are being attacked and when the missiles actually hit. It is *in this* time that the military has to decide whether an attack is under way, or whether the radar or computer is malfunctioning, or whether it has picked up a lost aircraft, a flock of geese, or radar echoes of the moon. In the last decade there have been low level nuclear alerts caused by each of these last four. When the response time is cut down then such decisions must be made more quickly. The result is to place nuclear detection systems on a hair-trigger and increase the possibilities of accidental nuclear war.

(c) The decrease in response time makes it very difficult to reach decisions, especially if the decision is supposed to be made by the head of state. This will increase the pressure to allow lower level officials to make a nuclear decision, and this too increases the likelihood of accidental nuclear war. An alternative strategy now being considered in order to cope with reduced response time is to turn over the whole mechanism of retaliation to a computerised 'launch-on-warning' system. In such a system a computer or, rather, a programme that someone has put into the computer, would scan the data and provide an automatic response. Such a system is, in fact, a doomsday weapon from out of *Doctor Strangelove* or *War Games*, and computers, especially the relatively primitive Russian ones, are notoriously unreliable things on which to stake the future of the earth.

(d) Newer generations of nuclear missiles, such as the Trident, the MX and the Pershing II are far more accurate than previous ones. This means that they could explode close enough (possibly within 120 metres for the Trident) to even a reinforced Soviet missile silo that they could destroy that missile. These missiles have the potential for a 'first-strike' capability, the ability to destroy Soviet missiles and leave the USSR unable to counter-attack. This would destroy Soviet deterrence and lead to the breakdown of the nuclear stand-off. Such a situation would tempt the Soviets to attack while they still could (either before an American launch or during the 'response time') or tempt the Americans to launch an attack on Soviet missiles to which the USSR could not respond. The possibility of nuclear war increases again.

(e) The cruise missile is small and easily transported. Hence it is easier to hide. This cuts down the possibility of monitoring them and thus reduces the possibility of verifiable multilateral disarmament. The cruise will make effective arms control and reduction very much harder.

Apart from these weapons developments there is the rapid proliferation of nuclear arms. We have stressed the confrontation between NATO and the Warsaw Pact but there is every indication that countries such as China, India, Pakistan, Brazil, Argentina, Israel, Libya, Iraq, Switzerland, and South Africa have or are developing nuclear capabilities. As the years pass by the possibility increases of nuclear war in any part of the world. Beyond this is the equally frightening possibility of terrorists acquiring a nuclear bomb.

The Limits of Security

The result of installing these newer weapons to increase 'security' is, in fact, to render everyone even more insecure and vulnerable. We are on a treadmill going nowhere. If we are truly concerned that governments should fulfil their God-given responsibility to protect their citizens then we must break out of the arms spiral. We must not install new weapons that end up making us and everyone else in the world more vulnerable. I am not denying the need for security; I am saying that military security itself demands a halt to this process.

Even beyond the question of whether the arms spiral threatens our security, we must question our goal of security itself. Security is, as we have said, a quite legitimate thing. But security is not above and beyond every other thing and it should not control our lives. We must put other considerations alongside it. We must be willing to accept limits on security on a search for security. If we fail to do this then we are confessing that security, not God, is our 'god'. This 'god' will then bind us and trap us. 'For whosoever would save his life will lose it; and whosoever loses his life for my sake will find it' (Mark 8:35). Hence it is imperative not only that we halt the nuclear arms spiral for our own security but also that we be willing even to lessen our security in order to achieve a more lasting peace. The only way to break out of an arms spiral is to break out of it, and that is what we must do. This will involve an element of risk, but installing new weapons systems seems to entail even greater risks. There seems to be no good reason to put off the day when we break out of the arms spiral and every reason not to delay. Consequently I would oppose the installation of cruise missiles, Pershing II's or Tridents.

CONCLUSIONS

Our discussion in this chapter leads us to conclude that while states are called to protect their legitimate interests, by force if necessary, this does not define their task. In international relations, governments should not be directed by 'national interest' but by a concern to act justly toward other countries. We must attempt to realise such just relations through international agreements and international law.

We must refuse to engage in nuclear war but we may accept a policy of nuclear deterrence while working towards enforced, inspected, multilateral nuclear disarmament. Such deterrence should lead us to recognise clearly that the only purpose in retaining nuclear weapons is to deter an enemy from launching a nuclear attack. We should dismantle many of our present nuclear weapons, replace nuclear weapons only with those which are safer from attack, not put in place any weapons that threaten an enemy's ability to maintain its own deterrent, seek arms control agreements with the Soviet Union, eschew any nuclear threats, and abandon NATO's 'first-strike' policy. If the abandonment of a first strike policy seems to lead to a genuine threat to western Europe by the Warsaw Pact then NATO defensive *conventional* forces must be made sufficiently strong in order to deter such an attack.[9]

The dynamics of the nuclear arms race reveal a fixation on military security which in turn tends to undermine any genuine security. Newer weapons threaten to undermine deterrence. It is imperative to stop this spiralling arms emplacement and this should be done by refusing to install weapons systems such as the cruise missile, the Pershing II missile and the Trident submarine. As security itself must not become an idol we must be willing to lessen our security to halt this race.

Most of these conclusions are negative ones, stressing what we must avoid. Our positive task must be one of *peacemaking*. We must move *toward* international agreements to stop the proliferation of nuclear weapons throughout the world. We must also negotiate arms control and reduction agreements with the Soviet Union working towards total, verifiable, multilateral disarmament. A unilateral *reduction* in our number of nuclear weapons would be a stimulant to this process.

7: Some Guides for Christian Action

A COMMUNAL TASK

Individualism

Many Christian discussions focus either on what the church should do or on what the individual Christian should do.[1] However I do not think that either of these options is really the most suitable avenue for Christian political service. I would like to show why this is the case, focussing first of all on the question of individual action.

It is a modern tendency to refer to people as 'individuals'. Often nothing more is meant by 'individuals' than by 'persons'. But the word 'individual' can have overtones that invariably convey more than this. Literally an 'individual' is an 'individuum', something which cannot be divided or, more specifically, an *atom*. If we talk about someone as an individual then we are talking of them as if they were a *separate* basic unit. Conceiving of people this way is conceiving of them as essentially *apart from* the *relationships* in which they exist. It suggests that human beings should be understood, in the first place, as being alone.

Christians are strongly affected by this tendency. Christian writings, especially evangelical ones, are full of references to 'the Christian and the labour union', 'the Christian and the university', 'the Christian and society' or 'the Christian and politics' as though individual Christians exercising their own personal responsibility is the primary concern. But such a way of thinking is not very biblical.

It must be emphasised that the individual, in the sense of the person, is vitally important. Each person is a unique centre of freedom and responsibility that should not and cannot be overridden. God is concerned for each person. We certainly should speak of personal salvation, personal faith, personal commitment, personal worth and personal responsibility, even and especially in politics. But, while we are indeed persons, we are not *individuals* in the sense that our actions, lives and responsibilities should be understood in a way separate from those of others. The Christian faith is utterly contrary to the rampant individualism of the western world (as well as to the collectivism of the East). We must understand that we are members of something, members of the body of Christ.

In an obvious extension of the meaning of Israel as a chosen nation, Peter writes to the exiled and dispersed Christian churches:

> You are a chosen race, a royal priesthood, a holy nation, God's own people, that you may declare the wonderful deeds of him who called you out of darkness into his marvellous light. Once you were no people but now you are God's people; once you had not received mercy but now you have received mercy. (1 Pet. 2:9–10)

Peter tells his readers that they are a nation, body of people with a specific identity *together*. Similarly, when Paul speaks about predestination or election, it is often the *nation* of Israel and the *body* of the church as predestined that receive his attention (cf. Romans 9; 11:28–32). We are not separated persons: we are members of a nation, members of the body of Christ. We are also told how this nation is supposed to function. It is a body and each of us are members (limbs) of it: 'We have many members, and all the members do not have the same function, so we . . . are . . . individually members one of another.' (Rom. 12:4–5). 'Now there are varieties of gifts . . . and varieties of service . . . for just as the body is one and has many members, and all the members of the body, though many, are one body, so it is with Christ. . . . God arranges the organs in the body, each one of them, as he chose . . . there are many parts but one body . . . Now you are the body of Christ and individually members of it.' (1 Cor. 12:4, 12, 18 20, 27).

We are individually members of a body. We are particular parts of a whole. Christ is represented on earth not by a lot of individuals who each fulfil all that he has commanded but by a body which, when fitted together, fulfils his word and represents him to humankind. Each of us is like an eye or an arm or a foot. To think of us being politically active as individuals is like urging a foot to go for a walk. Rather than this fragmented picture, each of us is to do a partial task, a task which is only accomplished when it is fitted together with the tasks of others. The same point is made by Jesus when he tells his disciples 'you are the salt of the earth' (Matt. 5:13). Salt in Israel was rock salt or else evaporates from the Dead Sea. It did not come in saltshakers nor in grains from a packet. It came in lumps which were for rubbing or packing around food to preserve it, or in bits which were broken off for seasoning. The analogy to salt is an analogy to the body.

All Christian action is in the first place the action of a body. Authentic Christian political action should not be the action of lone individuals but of a body. This is not to downgrade the actions of Christians who, to some degree on their own, have taken up political responsibilities and in many cases have done sterling service. We are simply pointing out that any authentic and effective Christian political action should be done as an inter-related part of the corporate action of members of the body of Christ. In fact those 'individual' Christians who *have* been politically effective have been so because in actual fact they were *not* lone individuals. They were tied in with groups who could and did agree and disagree with them, encourage them, give guidance to them, criticise them and keep them honest. People such as Lord Shaftesbury or William Wilberforce did not act alone, they were parts of a strong and essential network of Christians who took their allegiance to the gospel and to one another more seriously than they did a narrow allegiance to a party.

Hence, rather than speaking about 'the Christian and politics', we must speak about 'the body of Christ in its political expression.' This is especially true in the modern world where, in a massive and complex society, organised fields such as politics, education, science or industry require collective action. Unity of direction, teamwork and organisation are essential. It is naive to think that, except in the most unusual circumstances, isolated teachers can set the educational direction of the nation, or that isolated scientists can set the pattern of research, or that isolated workers can restructure the union or the factory, or that isolated politicians or political activists can redirect the nation. Effectiveness in these fields requires community and organisation.

The Church

Because of the pitfalls of individualism, it has become more common to emphasise that the *church* is the body that should act politically. Indeed, so common is this theme that when clergy or synods are criticised as going beyond their competence when they make political pronouncements they often respond by saying that the gospel is as wide as life itself. This response is most certainly true, but it avoids half of the criticism, for it conveys the implicit assumption that whatever the gospel requires should be done by the clergy. This view of the church as the Christian political agent has led to an increasing number of political pronouncements by synods and to an increasingly political clergy.

Another aspect of this identification of the church as the body that fulfils *all* the requirements of the gospel is the stress, particularly among evangelicals, on the church as an 'alternative community', an 'alternative culture', or even as an 'alternative society'.[2] The 'new nation' is thought to be the church, Christian service is to be carried out in the church, and the church is thought to manifest the ethics of Jesus Christ within itself. The church is the body that calls for and carries out justice, mercy and stewardship. The church community is Christ's political representative.

What should we make of this stress on the church as the agent of Christian politics? First of all we must say that it represents several positive developments, for certainly the church does have a political responsibility. The church is called to proclaim the Word of God and this Word speaks to all of life. Good preaching and synodical decisions must address all of God's world, including politics. As for the church as an alternative community, we should certainly move beyond the often disparate and alienated gatherings that many of us find each Sunday. The church must become a community that lives in such a way that those outside it say 'see how they love one another' and it must be a servant to those about it.

But despite these positive elements we must be careful about saying that the church is the Christian political avenue. One problem is the question of *competence*. Do clergy, or other church officers, have any ability to address political matters *simply by the fact that they hold leadership positions in the church*? I think not.[3] Nor is it possible to see how the church can be an alternative *society*. This may be possible in a rural setting but, in a city, churches, even if they are house communities, usually need to rely on the surrounding society for shelter, for food, for transportation, for income, for news, for tools and for most of the other things needed in order to live. And if a church is *dependent* on the surrounding society in order to survive, then it cannot pretend that it is an *alternative to* that society. To really be an alternative society it would need to do *within itself* everything that societies need to do. The church would need to grow crops, raise animals, make clothes, build buildings, make roads, manufacture steel and cars (or buses), engage in research, and so forth. A church which does not do all of these cannot claim that it is an alternative society, for it can only be *one part* of *God's world* and its service can only be one part of the service which ought to be rendered by the people of God.

When we put the matter in this way it becomes clearer that leadership in the church is not necessarily leadership in Christian politics, or leadership in Christian anything-else. Christian service is as wide as the creation itself. The new nation in Jesus Christ is to do anything that people can properly do, and it is to do it in a way that loves God and our neighbour. There is no more reason to expect the church to be *the* Christian political body than there is to expect the church to do research in plants, or manufacture computers or run airlines. But all these can be aspects of Christian service.

Varieties of 'Church'

Our discussion up to this point may seem confusing and even contradictory. I have emphasised that politics is not primarily an individual task but is one given to the *body* of Christ. Yet I have criticised many of the views that emphasise the *Church's* political task. What other alternative is there? However in some senses it is right to say that the church is the one that acts politically. It depends on what is meant by *church*. In order to clarify this we need to look at the various meanings of 'church'.

We use the word church to refer to a variety of things. It can mean a 'house of worship' (*kyriakos*), (as in 'I'm going down to the church') or a local congregation or community (*ekklesia*), (as in 'Which church are you going to join?') or a denomination (as in 'the Presbyterian Church') or 'the invisible body of Christ' (as in 'Christ died for the Church').

I will pass over these meanings and concentrate on one other meaning. We also use the word 'Church' referring to Christians considered together. We speak of, for example, 'the Church in the third world'. This does not mean the denominations *per se*, nor does it mean something invisible, it means Christians in the third world, those who in that part of the world have been called out by Jesus Christ. 'Church' understood this way includes Christian families, evangelistic organisations, student clubs, Christian publishers, music festivals and so on through the whole range of Christian activities. It includes the many and various activities which Christians engage in each day, buying and selling, labouring, making music, studying, sex, play, and so forth. In a real sense the Church is doing all these things. The denomination, the congregation, the people gathered for worship are only some aspects of *this* Church, they are not its totality. It has other aspects as wide as the creation itself. It is the Church understood in this wider way that should be politically active.

Christian Political Groups

Politics is not primarily for individual Christians nor is it primarily for denominational bodies or local congregations. Rather it is a task for a body of Christians who collectively take up this one aspect of the Church's overall ministry. We need to form Christian communities and organisations whose explicit goal is political service. We need corporate Christian political expressions distinct from the institutional churches.

Occasionally people characterise the view that we should form Christian organisations as one of retreat from the world. Surely Christians should be 'out there' and not in their own ghettoes. But, while there is certainly a place for individual witness, the whole point of our discussion so far is that in politics we need more than an individual witness. A Christian corporate expression is not a holy huddle, it is a *way of going out* in the world. It is a way of 'being involved' *together*. The biblical stress is on a *corporate* witness.

In any case most Christians do make a corporate witness in many areas of their life, often without realising it. We have Christian festivals, Christian publishers, Christian art groups, Christian study groups, Christian professional groups. Why do we have them? Because we have realised that each of us, on our own, can do very little. Very few of us are geniuses, heroines or heros. We need to build things *together* so that our work can be gifts to the world. This is especially true in our political work.

This position is sometimes also characterised as *divisive* because it could set Christians off against each other or against non-Christians. But there is no reason why creating Christian political groups need be more divisive than anything else. Nearly all politics takes place through groups so, willy-nilly, politically active Christians will have *some* group identity that sets them off from other people anyway. Such groups can be divisive or they can try to give contributions and service which are appreciated by others, or they can do both depending on the circumstances. But, even if such groups *were* divisive, that should not *per se* cause us to shy away from them. Individual witness can be divisive too. In fact the gospel can be divisive. Jesus also said 'Do you think I come to bring peace on earth? No, I tell you, but rather division . . . they will be divided father against son and son against father' (Luke 12:51–53). The gospel divides even as it unites. As Christians we should have no fear of being different, even politically different.

In advocating the formation of Christian political groups I am not advocating the formation of a Christian political party. I do not think there is any *in principle* reason why we should not do so, it is certainly not forbidden by the gospel and it could become necessary. But I do not think this is the time or the place to do so. With present realities such a party would be quixotic or ideological. To be worthwhile it would require an alienation from present parties and a widespread Christian political consciousness that does not exist now. Hence it is doubtful that such a party would be useful in realising any authentic Christian goals in the near future.

The actual types of groups that should be developed depend on a whole variety of circumstances. They could be adjuncts of local churches, or local neighbourhood organisations, or lobbying groups, or research groups, or caucuses inside other organisations or in existing political parties. But what is essential is that such groups have a Christian identity and direction, that they do not reduce the gospel to one of the current political ideologies but seek consistently to develop and push for policies that come from the uniqueness of the gospel. As long as this is maintained then we can be allies and co-workers with others who agree on the issue at hand, whether that be nuclear disarmament, pornography, or economic policy.

Apart from Christian action groups we need people, centres and organisations which are devoted to political study and analysis (here the Shaftesbury project is a good example). It means that we should try to develop Christian magazines and journals which are devoted not just to theology and church news but to reporting and analysing the news of the day with Christian insight.

Maintaining the Christian character of a political group, whether on a local or national basis, is no easy task. Seeking to preserve one's identity can easily degenerate into a static dogmatism guided more by the fear of doing something wrong than by the hope of doing something right. On the other hand, activists (and who in politics is anything else!) often will find such Christian identity frustrating. For one thing such Christian groups are bound to be small at the beginning, composed of people with widely different views. They will be abstract, vague and divided in their political opinions, simply because they do not have the years of accumulated political experience, reflection and analysis that other political groups have. The temptation for activists in such a situation is always that 'the grass is greener on the other side of the hill'. Secular political groupings are more active, are better connected, have a clearer idea of what they want, are practical and, most important, have a chance to actually get things done and make a difference. Furthermore, secular groups often have a much better grasp of and commitment to justice than do Christian groups. In such a situation, the temptation to forsake a Christian political identity is hardly rampant wickedness and is hard to resist, but resisted it must be. We should certainly join with and cooperate with others but, if what we have said in this book is true, then the gospel is ultimately the only source of political hope: we must maintain a community that seeks to live by it.

Local Church Support

While I have stressed that the local church is not the primary political organ, yet such churches have a vital role if any real Christian political service is to be done. This could include the more mundane things like providing meeting space, making announcements in the church bulletin, and providing legitimacy by giving an endorsement from the clergy. But perhaps most important are two other things. The first is good preaching – preaching that assumes we live more than private lives or lives in the institutional church. We do not need preaching that portrays the institutional church as the centre and goal of Christian activity, but preaching that sees the church as a centre of encouragement and direction for the Christian work that takes place every day of the week, in factories and schools and meeting rooms, the tasks that occupy the best energies and most of the waking hours of the members of the body of Christ. We need preaching that directs us and gives us hope in what we do on Monday morning and on Saturday night.

This does not particularly mean activist sermons on El Salvador or the latest Tory budget, although these are as appropriate as areas of sermon application as is any philandering in the congregation. It means biblical exposition, without fear or favour, on (if we focus on politics) the meaning of justice, the task of government, authority, stewardship, mercy, jubilee, war, poverty, property, and so on and so forth. A church which takes up this task seriously will not commit the error of making itself a political body and it will ultimately do more for politics through the lay activity it provokes and ignites than will any number of denominational committees.

A second important task of the local church relevant to politics is the depth of community it provides. Politics is tiring, dispiriting and corrupting work. Its practitioners need loving support and criticism. Being married to political activists is notoriously difficult so, unless we resurrect the ideal of celibacy (perhaps a good idea in many cases) we need major marriage and parenting supports. Political activity takes time and that means, for most of us, portions of our rather small 'free time'. However local church groups can, by pooling goods and services, free up people emotionally and financially for political service. Many of the charismatic congregations in Britain take this sort of commitment seriously. If they could overcome their reluctance to see politics as ministry, then they could provide a great and exciting base for political work.

Obedience not Goals

Because of the nature of idolatry we must beware of thinking that Christian politics primarily presents a set of goals or provides a blueprint for a new political order. We must beware of either of these for they can easily cause us to turn away from one idol in order to embrace another. Our new goals, whether they be equality of income or eradication of pornography, can easily become dominating forces to which everything else is subordinated and by which everything else is judged. We must remember that an idol is a *good thing* in creation which is made into a god. A blueprint, or even a goal, can neglect the factor of historical change and become fixed or rigid so that its implementation becomes unjust. An idol is a 'graven image', it is *carved in stone*: our response to God, which is what our politics is, should never itself be carved in stone.

All programmes for an ideal society must be treated sceptically. The fact that we seek to offer a Christian approach to politics is no guarantee of success. From the Constantinian hope of a Christian Empire, to the Puritan 'city set on a hill' in New England, to the Jesuit state of Paraguay, to the utopian communes of the nineteenth and twentieth centuries, the history of Christendom is littered with failed political dreams. Christian politics is not magic, it cannot provide easy, clear and simple solutions. It is simply taking up our responsibility before God to try to establish just relations between us.

Rather than *goals to be achieved*, we should try to outline *ways to be followed*. We should pay political heed to Jesus' admonitions on mammon in the Sermon on the Mount.

Therefore I tell you, do not be anxious about your life, what you shall eat or what you shall drink, nor about your body, what you shall put on. Is not life more than clothing? . . . But if God so clothes the grass of the field, which today is alive and tomorrow is thrown into the oven, will he not much more clothe you, O ye of little faith. . . . But *seek first* his kingdom and his righteousness, and all these things shall be yours as well. Therefore do not be anxious for tomorrow for tomorrow will be anxious for itself. Let the day's own trouble be sufficient for the day. (Matt. 6:25–34, emphasis added).

The things that Jesus tells us not to be anxious about are not bad things. They are things we need and ought to have. But he says that being anxious for them, striving for them, will not help. Instead we are told to *seek first* the kingdom of God and God's justice and these other things will follow from that. Jesus' words are a direct rebuke to every kind of idolatry. He does not set forth goals but describes a way to be followed of daily seeking justice and he promises that God's blessing will follow from this. Blessing is never a result of work but a *fruit of obedience*.

What Jesus says is also shown in the world about us. Political results – and not only them – are incalculable. Despite the dreams of futurologists and 'policy scientists' armed with computers, we simply do not and cannot control either the future or the outcome of our decisions. The diplomat George F. Kennan, a deeply committed Christian, has described this phenomenon in detail in his studies of foreign policy. He maintains that pragmatic policies, designed to secure some national interest, often produce the opposite of what was intended. Consequently, he claims that a concern for honesty, constitutionality, due process of law, and a commitment to moral principles is itself the best long-term and short-term foreign policy.[4]

Our political task is not one guaranteed of success. It is not even oriented to such success. Instead it is taking up a path of obedience to God in the problems that confront us, hour by hour, and decade by decade. This does not mean we should not use foresight nor plan ahead. But it does mean that we should not attempt to freeze the world into our mould or fix a definite future. It also means that we should not forsake our path in order to achieve political power. If we need to give up what we believe in order to reach or maintain a position of power, then that power can never be used to achieve what we believe in.

POSTSCRIPT: CHRISTIAN POLITICS BETWEEN THE TIMES

The biblical picture of a 'new heaven and a new earth' should not cause us to be overconfident in our service. It is true that our task spans the entire creation. It is true that we will see new heavens and a new earth. It is true that in Jesus Christ the power of sin has already been overcome. He said 'Be of good cheer, I have overcome the world' (John 16:33). But the completion of this great redemption awaits his return. Jesus said 'Be of good cheer' to the disciples because he had just told them 'In the world you have tribulation'. He warned them 'Do not think that I have come to bring peace on earth; I have not come to bring peace but a sword' (Matt. 10:34).

We cannot expect our work to be easy nor can we expect it to be always welcomed with open arms. But our actions in God's earth are not futile, they are not whiling away the hours for something that will ultimately count for nothing and will be destroyed at the last day. When Peter writes that 'the heavens and earth that now exist have been stored up for fire' (2 Pet. 3:7), he draws an explicit parallel to the destruction of the world by water at the time of Noah (vv. 5–6). Peter is saying that the order of this age and world, an order which is opposed to God, will pass away, but that works of righteousness, as with Noah, will remain. The image is of the refiner's fire which separates the pure from the impure (cf. Jer. 9:7; Isa. 48:10; Luke 12:49; Rev. 1:15), the fire which burns up the chaff (Matt. 3:12) and leaves the good wheat to be gathered in the barn of the Lord (Matt. 13:24–30; see also 2 Pet 3:10 on 'uncovering sin'). In Isaiah's closing prophecy his vision leaps ahead to see the future of Israel in terms of God's ultimate plans and he weaves all these themes together:

For behold, the Lord will come in fire, and his chariots like the stormwind, to render his anger in fury, and his rebuke in flames of fire. For by fire will the Lord execute judgment, and by his sword upon all flesh; and those slain by the Lord shall be many . . . and I am coming to gather all nations and tongues, and they shall come and see my glory . . . and they shall declare my glory among the nations. And they shall bring all your brethren from all the nations as an offering to the Lord, upon horses, and in chariots, and in litters, and upon mules, and upon dromedaries, to my holy mountain Jerusalem, says the Lord, just as the Israelites bring their offerings in a clear vessel to the house of the Lord. . . . For as the new heavens and the new earth which I will make shall remain before me says the Lord; so shall your descendants and your name remain . . . (Isa. 66:15, 16, 18, 19, 20, 22)

That which is good and just will be purified and that which is evil and unjust will be destroyed.

We do not live now in a time of perfection and completeness.

Nor do we live in a time when the kingdom of God is extinct. We live in the time before the final winnowing, the time when the wheat and the tares continue to grow together. We cannot and should not expect any immediate victory over evil, but we can expect what the late Francis Schaeffer has called 'substantial healing' – real changes and real fruits of peace and love.

As we look at the world about us we see increasing numbers of people starving, and an increase in the means of feeding people. We see the development of weapons that can end the world, and of communications that can help unify the world. We live in a century that has perfected the art of genocide, and also proclaims a 'Universal Declaration of Human Rights'. Our world sways with the contradictory currents of God's preserving hand and humankind's recurrent evil.

If we consider the Church then we find the same contradictions holding sway. In a world of starvation we have Christian books on how to lose weight. Many followers of the Prince of Peace, who claim a spiritual warfare, insist that only weapons and armaments can protect christendom. Preachers proclaim that Jesus Christ is the Lord of all creation, but then treat most of that creation as if it were alien to the word of the gospel.

In this century we live in the greatest age of missionary expansion in the history of the Church. Despite our sins, the number of Christians increases vastly. The gospel spreads forth quickly over continents. But along with this expansion, we have suffered from an inner contraction. When faced with political problems in their lands, the children trained in mission schools are forced to turn elsewhere for guidance, to the ideologies of Marxism, liberalism or conservatism. In many parts of the world the only notable political impact of Christianity has been as an ideology of a privileged Christian elite. In other places, because of the Christian belief that history is not cyclical but is actually going somewhere, it has provided a seedbed for the growth of Marxism that traditional cultures could not provide.

The impact of Christianity is now lessening in the industrial lands of the North Atlantic and growing in the 'third world'. In this we can rejoice a little, for the fate of Christianity is now no longer tied to the fate of western culture. But we should also feel shame about this, because it is a sign that we have not seen the implications of the gospel in our own lands. Our ability to lead our society in ways of blessing is sadly diminished.

But this process is not irreversible. Christianity is the religion of new birth, new life, new beginnings. The hand of the Lord is not shortened and it may stretch forth over us again. We have much to do. Our world suffers, waiting for the healing of Jesus

Christ. We have of ourselves no strength or power. We kid ourselves if we pretend that we do, or think that large numbers will carry the day. Nor, in an age which has produced Auschwitz and Cambodia, dare we to be too joyful in our politics.

But, in so far as we hear the Word of God and in so far as we humbly and patiently seek to do God's will, then we can have strength and hope. We have hope because God's promises will come to fruition, and we will see a new heavens and a new earth.

So, in this 'between times', as we await the coming of the Kingdom, let us fight evil, pain and suffering, even in politics. Let us expect, and work toward, and pray for that day when the voice cries:

Behold the dwelling of God is with them. He will dwell with them, and they shall be his people, and God himself will be with them; He will wipe away every tear from their eyes, and death shall be no more, neither shall there be mourning nor crying nor pain anymore, for the former things have passed away. (Rev. 21:3, 4)

The kingdom of the world has become the kingdom of our Lord and of his Christ, and he shall reign for ever and ever. (Rev. 11:15)

Behold, I make all things new. (Rev. 21:5)

Notes

Preface

1. Philip Giddings, 'What is Good Government' (Nottingham: Shaftesbury Project, 1976), p. 1.

Chapter 1: Introduction

1. (Mount Vernon, N. Y.; Peter Pauper Press, 1958), p. 48.
2. R. H. Tawney, *The Acquisitive Society* (London: Collins, 1961), p. 11.
3. J. M. Keynes, *The General Theory of Employment, Interest and Money* (London: MacMillan, 1973), pp. 383–4.
4. Frances Ferrarotti, 'A Conversation with György Lukacs' pp. 30–34 *Worldview* (May, 1972), p. 32.

Chapter 2: Christian Action in God's World

1. This discussion of the cultural mandate relies heavily on Al Wolters 'The Foundational Command: Subdue the Earth' (Toronto: Institute for Christian studies, 1973).
2. I have discussed Christian views of work in my 'Vocation, Work and Jobs', in P. Marshall et al. *Labour of Love: Essays on Work* (Toronto: Wedge, 1980), pp. 1–19.
3. Martin Luther, *Works* vol. 21 (St. Louis: Concordia, 1956), p. 237.
4. William Tyndale, 'A Parable of the Wicked Mammon' (1927) in *Doctrinal Treatises and Portions of Holy Scripture* (Cambridge: Parker Society, 1848), p. 98.
5. The Revised Standard Version reads 'Do not be conformed to this world. . . .' (12:2) but 'world' can be more accurately translated as 'age'. One possible objection to what I am saying here about service in and reconciliation of the *world* is the frequent scriptural denunciations of the 'world'. Paul says in 1 Corinthians 7:31 '(let) . . . those who deal with the world (deal) as though they had no dealings with it. For the form of this world is passing away.' In the parable of the sower Jesus tells how

some seed is choked through the 'cares of the world' (John 18:36). James tells us to keep ourselves 'unstained from the world' (James 1:27) John tells us we are 'not of the world' (John 15:19). These examples could be multiplied but they do not contradict the teaching about the reconciliation of the world. 'World' in the Bible has several meanings. One meaning refers to the way humans have sinfully ordered the world, especially the social order. This is the meaning in the verses we have just quoted. Another meaning refers to geography or territory, as in 'this gospel will be preached throughout the whole world' (Matt. 24:14). A third meaning of world is the *created order*, what God has made for us to live in. This is the world we are referring to, the world that will be reconciled, for Jesus came 'not to condemn the world, but that the world might be saved through him' (John 3:17). Thus there is no contradiction between John saying 'do not love the world . . .' (1 John 2:15) and John recording Jesus saying 'For God so loved the world . . .' (John 3:16).

6. Herman Bavinck, 'Christ and Christianity', *The Biblical Review* vol. 1 (1916), p. 217.

7. Quotations from a report on the conference by David Bosch and Chris Sugden, *Themelios* vol. 8, no. 2 (January 1983), pp. 26–7. See also R. J. Sider, *Evangelism, Salvation and Social Justice* with a response by John R. W. Stott, (Bramcote: Grove Books, 2nd Edition, 1977).

8. Calvin, *Institutes* I. 16. 3; André Biéler, *La pensée économique et sociale de Calvin*, (Geneva: Librairie de l'Université, 1961), p. 321.

Chapter 3: Politics in God's World

1. This discussion of Cain and Lamech is derived from Meredith G. Kline, 'Oracular Origin of the State', in G. Tuttle, ed., *Biblical and Near Eastern Studies* (Grand Rapids: Eerdmans, 1978), pp. 132–41.

2. Cf. G. von Rad, *Genesis; A Commentary* (London: SCM, 1961), p. 102. See also C. J. H. Wright, *Human Rights: A Study in Biblical Themes* (Bramcote: Grove Books, 1979), pp. 9f.

3. H. J. Boeker, *Law and the Administration of Justice in the Old Testament and Near East*, trans. J. Moiser (London: S.P.C.K., 1981), pp. 40ff. The Israelites themselves were probably clearer on this matter for there was a 'book of the kingdom'. Psalm 72 may be a reflection of this 'book'.

4. John Howard Yoder writes that 'it is inconceivable that these two verses [12:19 and 13:4] using such similar language should be meant to be read independently of one another.' *The Politics of Jesus* (Grand Rapids: Eerdmans, 1972), p. 199. I think this is true. However Yoder draws the conclusion from these verses that, as the Christian cannot take vengeance, 'the function exercised by government is not the function to be exercised by Christians.' Yoder does not allow the distinction between, on the one hand, Christians acting on their own authority and, on the other hand, Christians acting with the God-given authority of political office. I believe that unless this distinction is maintained then any idea of a political order at all would be lost. We would be left only with the assertion of personal will and power.

5. John 18:36 should not be read as saying 'not *of* this world' as though Jesus' kingdom is present only in another world. It is better translated as 'not *from* [Gr. 'εκ] this world order'. Jesus' power does not derive from the established world order but comes *into* it and transforms it. See also footnote 5 of chapter 2.

6. Cf. Boeker, op. cit. For a simpler introduction see C. J. H. Wright *Peace and Justice in the Bible* (Nottingham: Shaftesbury Project, n.d.).

7. The judges' impartiality in the Old Testament also extends to judgments between those who are Israelites and those who are not, between those in the covenant and those who are not. God's justice extends to *all* people (cf. Deut. 23:7; Ezek. 16:49; Amos 1; 2; 9:7). This is not a theme which I have developed in this book, but it would seem to imply, in the modern age, an impartiality on the part of governments between the claims of Christians and non-Christians.

8. Emil Brunner, *Justice and the Social Order* (London: Lutterworth, 1945), p. 89. See also my *Human Rights Theories in Christian Perspective* (Toronto: Institute for Christian Studies, 1983) pp. 17–23, and B. Zylstra 'The Bible, Justice and the State', *International Reformed Bulletin*, No. 55 (1973), pp. 2–18.

9. The following discussion is based on my 'Getting What You Vote For', a Political Service Bulletin' of Citizens for Public Justice, Toronto, February, 1981.

Chapter 4: Understanding the Modern World

1. G. Wenham, 'Law and the Legal System in the Old Testament' in B. Kaye and G. Wenham, eds., *Law, Morality and the Bible* (Leicester: Inter-Varsity Press, 1978), pp. 24–52.

2. For a brief analysis see my 'Christian Faith and Marxist Faith', *Vanguard*, October 1978, pp. 8–11. See also Andrew Kirk, *Liberation Theology: An Evangelical View from the Third World* (London: Marshall, Morgan and Scott, 1979). Probably the best introductory text written by an exponent of the theology of liberation is still Gustav Gutierrez, *A Theology of Liberation* (London: S.C.M., 1974).

3. Ellul, 'Epilogue: On Dialectic', pp. 291–308 of C. C. Christians and J. M. van Hook, eds., *Jacques Ellul: Interpretive Essays* (Urbana: University of Illinois Press, 1981), p. 292.

4. See F. Catherwood, 'Appendix: The Weber-Tawney Thesis' in his *The Christian in Industrial Society* (Leicester: Inter-Varsity 1980).

5. Cf. J. Falwell, 'A Look at Government Today', pp. 59–70 of his *Listen America!* (New York: Doubleday, 1980).

6. There are various attempts, although still primitive ones, to develop social analysis in the light of the gospel. See, for example, Alan Storkey, *A Christian Social Perspective* (Leicester: Inter-Varsity Press, 1979); Ilkley Study Group, *Christian Commitment and the Study of Sociology* (Leicester: Ilkley Study Group/UCCF, 1976); D. Lyon, *Christians and Sociology*, (Leicester: Inter-Varsity, 1975); B. Goudzwaard, *Capitalism and Progress* (Toronto and Grand Rapids: Wedge and Eerdmans, 1979); 'Toward Reformation in Economics' (Toronto: Institute for Christian

Studies, 1980). By far the most ambitious attempt of this kind is the work of the Dutch Christian philosopher, Herman Dooyeweerd. Dooyeweerd has been a major influence on several of the writers we have just listed. Dooyeweerd's major work in English is his *New Critique of Theoretical Thought*, 4 vols., (Philadelphia: Presbyterian and Reformed, 1953) (2nd Edition 1969). For Dooyeweerd's comments on sociology see especially chapter 8 of his *Roots of Western Culture* (Toronto: Wedge, 1979).

7. This expression was coined by H. Evan Runner. Its implications are sketched out in H. Vander Goot, ed., *Life is Religion* (St. Catherines, Ontario: Paideia Press, 1981) which was a *festschrift* dedicated to Runner.

8. The theme of idolatry is explored in relation to the family in Tony Walters *A Long Way from Home: A Sociological Exploration of Contemporary Idolatry* (Exeter: Paternoster, 1979).

9. B. Goudzwaard, *Aid for the Overdeveloped West* (Toronto, Wedge, 1975), pp. 14–15. Goudzwaard develops the meaning of idolatry and discusses the modern idols of 'nation', 'revolution', 'material prosperity', and 'guaranteed security' in his *Hope in a World Possessed: Repenting of Ideology and Idolatry* (Downer's Grove: Inter Varsity Press, 1984).

10. See the discussions by K. Grimwade in his 'A Christian Critique of Modern Revolution' (Nottingham: Shaftesbury Project, 1978) and by H. Evan Runner, *Scriptural Religion and Political Task* (Toronto, Wedge, 1974). On the more explicitly religious dynamics of revolutionary movements, see Christopher Dawson, *The Gods of Revolution* (New York: Minerva Press, 1975).

11. Quoted in the Toronto *Globe and Mail*, Oct. 1, 1983.

12. It is not my purpose here to deal with the question of 'right to life'. Instead, I am trying to illustrate a way of approaching the question of abortion. A good brief discussion on the issue of the status of the fetus is Oliver O'Donovan, *The Christian and the Unborn Child* (Bramcote: Grove Books, 1975). O'Donovan acknowledges, but does not address, the complex political difficulties that abortion raises.

13. I would also suggest that abortion should be by choice of the mother when her life or health is at stake. In the case of rape or incest we have to ask whether someone who has had pregnancy forced upon her should be *forced* to bear the cost of the life of another. The question is analagous to whether we would *force* someone to donate their lung or liver to someone who will die without it. I would say 'no' to both questions. I should also add that, as a male I have not and cannot experience and, hence, really understand many aspects of abortion.

Chapter 5: Economics and the Welfare State

1. This section relies on B. Goudzwaard, *Aid for the Overdeveloped West* (Toronto: Wedge, 1975), chapter 2.

2. Anthony Crosland, *The Future of Socialism* (London: Jonathan Cape, 1980), chapter xvi. Mrs Thatcher quoted in A. Sampson *The Changing Anatomy of Britain* (London: Hodder and Stoughton, 1982), p. 67.

3. J. K. Galbraith, *The New Industrial State* (Harmondsworth: Penguin, 1968), p. 162.

4. J. M. Keynes *Essays in Persuasion* (London: Macmillan, 1972), p. 331.

5. Galbraith, op. cit., p. 398.

6. See my 'What is Quality of Life', *Catalyst* (March 1981), pp. 7–11.

7. R. Easterlin, 'Does Money Buy Happiness?', *The Public Interest*, vol. 60 (Winter, 1973), pp. 3–10.

8. Fred Hirsch, *The Social Limits to Growth* (London: Routledge, 1977).

9. See John V. Taylor's brilliant *Enough is Enough* (London: S.C.M., 1975). The working papers of the World Council of Churches on a 'just, participatory and sustainable society' are also important on this point.

10. This understanding of present government policy as a 'two-track' approach was formulated by Stanley Carlson-Thies in his *Groping towards an Understanding of the Roles of Canadian Governments in Promoting and Distorting Wellbeing* (Toronto: Citizens for Public Justice, 1977).

11. The following discussion is based on my 'Justice for the Poor', *Political Service Bulletin* of Citizens for Public Justice, Toronto, August 1980.

12. For this reason it can be misleading to talk about 'an option for the poor' or a 'bias for the poor'. Such expressions imply only supporting one side in a conflict, and imply that the rich are beyond considerations of justice. In the Scriptures there is not a side but a standard, justice, by which conflicts are judged and which points to what relations should be like. In terms of this standard we seek to rectify injustice and such rectifying will, of course, mean the defending and redeeming of the poor. See also George Vandervelde 'Liberation and Redemption', *Vanguard*, October 1978, pp. 15–16.

13. A good beginning has been made by Bob Goudzwaard in his 'Toward Reformation in Economics', (Toronto: Institute for Christian Studies, 1980).

Chapter 6: International Relations and Nuclear Arms

1. This section relies on B. Zylstra's 'The Society of the Future in Political Perspective', paper presented at the Annual Meeting of the Canadian Sociological and Anthropological Association, Halifax, May 28, 1981.

2. James Skillen's *International Politics and the Demand for Global Justice* (Sioux Center, Iowa and Burlington, Ontario: Dordt College and G. R. Welch, 1981) is a good guide to these issues by a Christian international relations theorist.

3. J. H. Yoder, 'The "New Look" of the Just War Tradition', Mennonnite Central Committee (USA) *Peace Section Newsletter*, vol. 13, No. 2. May/June 1983.

4. For a brief introduction to deterrence, see McGeorge Bundy, 'The Bishops and the Bomb', *New York Review of Books*, June 16, 1983, pp. 3–8.

5. George F. Kennan 'The Atomic Bomb and the Choices for American Policy' (1950), in his *The Nuclear Debate* (New York: Pantheon, 1982), pp. 3–6.

6. These considerations are similar to those in *The Challenge of Peace: God's Promise and Our Response*, 'Pastoral Letter of the U.S. Catholic Bishops on War and Peace' (National Catholic News Service, May 19, 1983). This pastoral letter, which is one of the greatest contributions any Christian church has made to wrestling with the problem of nuclear arms, says that deterrence can be accepted provisionally but not as a long-term strategy. The only acceptable long-term strategy is complete nuclear disarmament (cf. p. 18).

Part of the reason the Bishops are wary of deterrence is that they believe deterrence implies a willingness to wage nuclear war, i.e. to retaliate if attacked. They also believe that to intend to do something sinful must itself be sinful. Hence, if, as the Bishops maintain, it is a sin to wage nuclear war then it must also be a sin to *intend* to wage nuclear war and therefore deterrence involves sinful intentions. I do not believe the Bishops are correct in saying this. If deterrence *is* a way of preventing nuclear war, as both the Bishops and I have said it is, then preparing to fight a nuclear war would be a means of preventing such a war, a means of preventing evil. Hence we reach the paradoxical position that an intention to commit evil is a way of avoiding that evil. This is a troubling position but not, on the face of it, I think, immoral. See the brief comments of Lewis Smedes 'Preparing to Destroy the World to Save it', *Reformed Journal* vol. 33, No. 5, May 1983, pp. 2–3.

7. See Lord Solly Zuckerman's *Nuclear Illusion and Reality* (London: Collins, 1982).

8. On this see McG. Bundy, G. F. Kennan, R. S. McNamara and G. Smith, 'Nuclear Weapons and the Atlantic Alliance' *Foreign Affairs*, vol. 60, No. 4 (1982), pp. 753–768.

9. I have repeatedly said '*if* NATO needs more to deter a Soviet attack'. This is because I have not dealt with this question here and so leave it open.

Chapter 7: Some Guides for Christian Action

1. Cf. John Gladwin's *God's People in God's World: Biblical Motives for Social Involvement* (Leicester: Inter-Varsity Press, 1979), chapters 9 and 11.

2. This is a particular stress in Anabaptist circles. See, for example, the writings of Jim Wallis.

3. Clergy may of course be competent for any number of other reasons, but there is nothing in the training and task of church leadership which itself provides any ability to exercise political leadership. It may not be stretching the point to consider whether this emphasis on the Church and politics is not also another attempt by the clergy to maintain their position of dominance in Christian affairs. On this see Richard Mouw's *Called to Holy Worldliness* (Philadelphia: Fortress Press, 1980), especially chapter 2, 'Theology and the Laity'.

4. George F. Kennan, 'Foreign Policy and Christian Conscience', *Atlantic* (May 1959), p. 44, quoted in J. H. Yoder, *The Christian Witness to the State* (Newton, Kansas: Faith and Life Press, 1964), p. 44.